This Book is Brad's

Design Elements 3

A Visual Reference by
Richard Hora
Mies Hora

The Art Direction Book Company, New York

Dedicated to Dee
and to all those who utilize this book.

Book design by Richard and Mies Hora
Special thanks to
Lou Dorfsman and W. Thomas Overgard
for their generous assistance.

Art Direction Book Company
10 East 39th Street
New York, New York 10016

Library of Congress Catalog Card Number 81–66127
International Standard Book Number 0–910158–97–7

Forward

The design elements in this collection are all arranged for your convenience. The material was selected from a wide variety of sources, both old and new, with many created specifically for this volume. It is organized into specific categories to speed search-and-find. Each design element was carefully selected for quality and general usefulness. All are generously sized for reproduction purposes. This book represents over forty years of collection and use, beginning as a working tool and eventually developing into a labor of love. We hope you find Design Elements 3 to be the inspirational and easy-to-use source file that we intended.

Richard Hora
Mies Hora

Introduction

A writer controls the content and elegance of his prose. Nevertheless, he is still at the mercy of his vocabulary.

He can play with ideas, juggle ideas or parody ideas. He can sculpt paragraphs and say anything he feels like saying. But he can do none of this without words. They are his raw material, the source of his inspiration, the tools of his trade.

A designer is not unlike a writer. His "words" are the graphic elements, symbols and signs which make up our common visual vocabulary.

Design Elements 3, like its excellent predecessors, is an invaluable graphic reference work. It builds upon the sturdy foundation of the first two volumes, and expands the designer's vocabulary even further to include a vast array of dingbats, patterns, unique borders and the elements to make up unusual borders.

This extraordinary series of books provides the designer with a much needed dictionary of images, a comprehensive resource for fine, reproduction quality ornaments and figures. Its immense practical value is matched only by its fine craftsmanship.

Lou Dorfsman
Vice President, Creative Director
Advertising & Design
CBS Inc.

Contents

Forward
Introduction

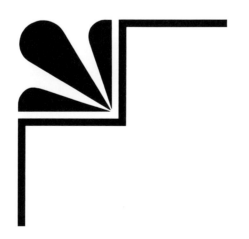

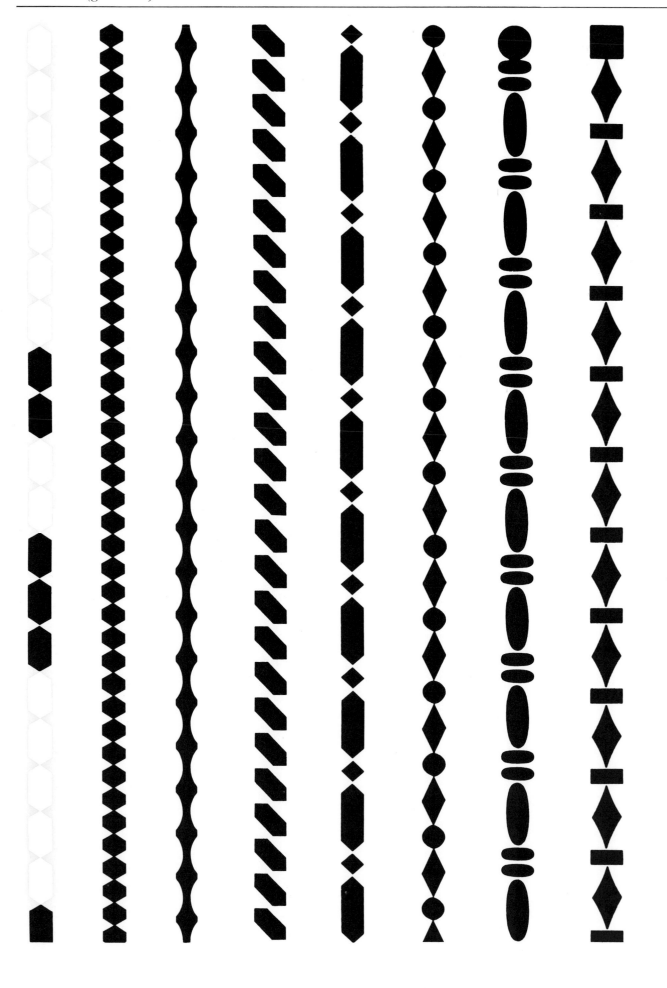

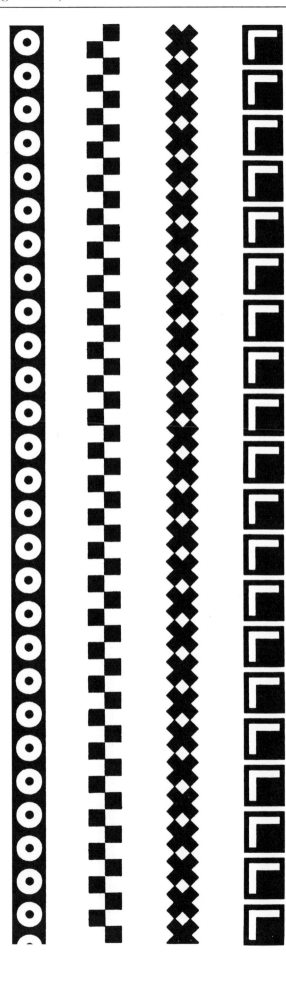
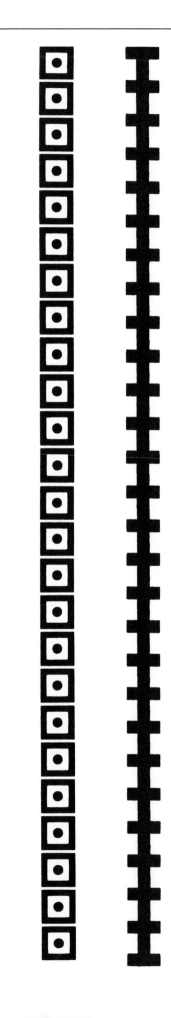

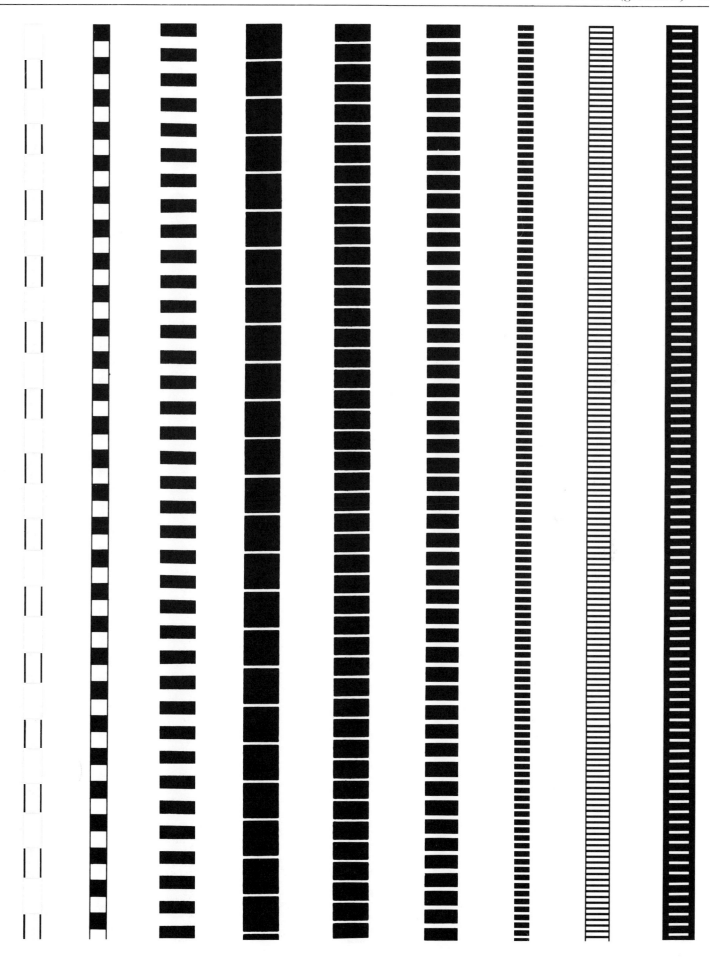

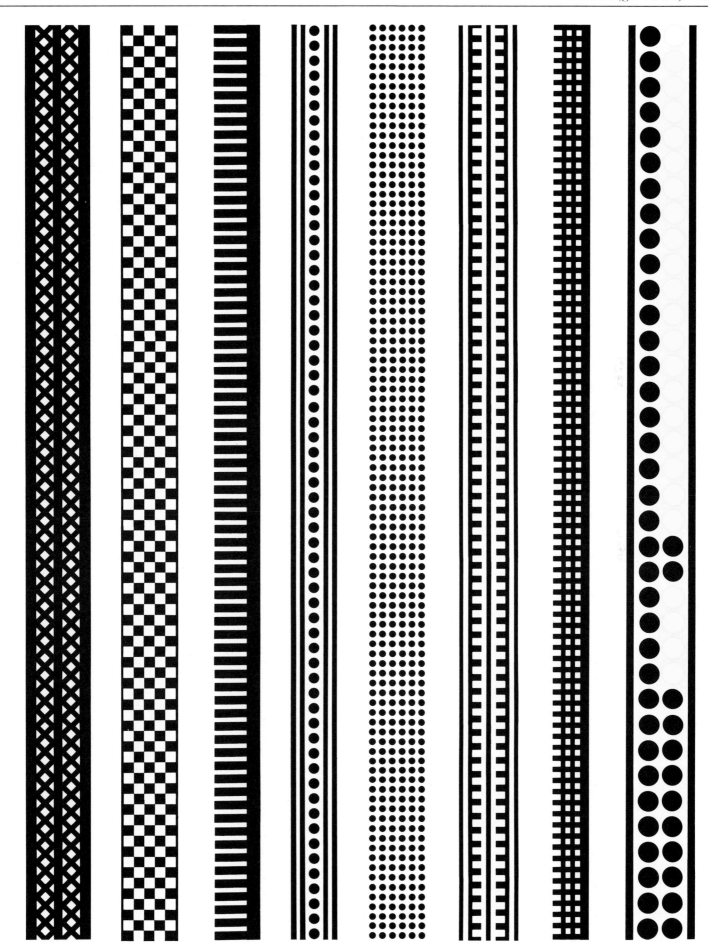

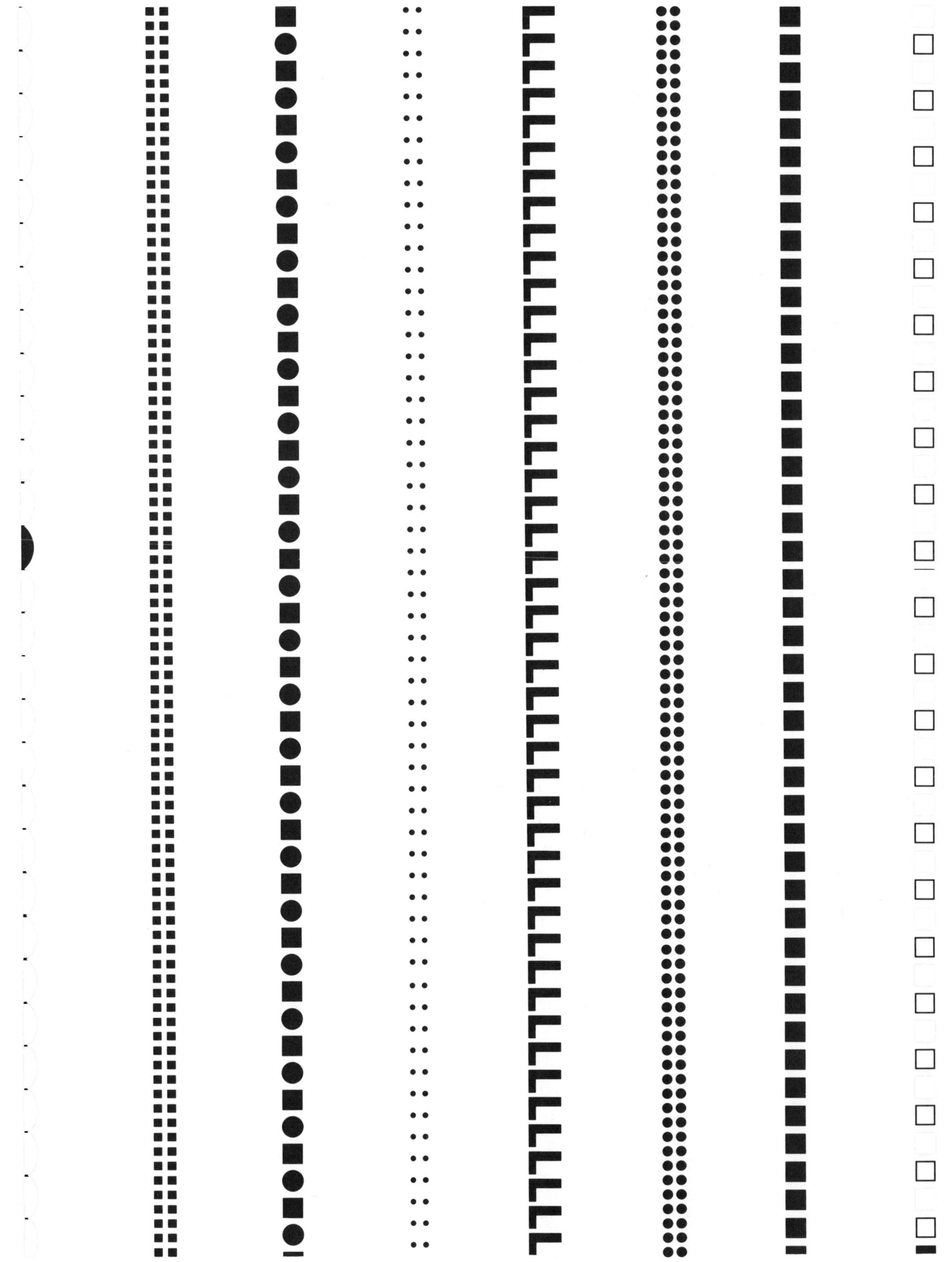

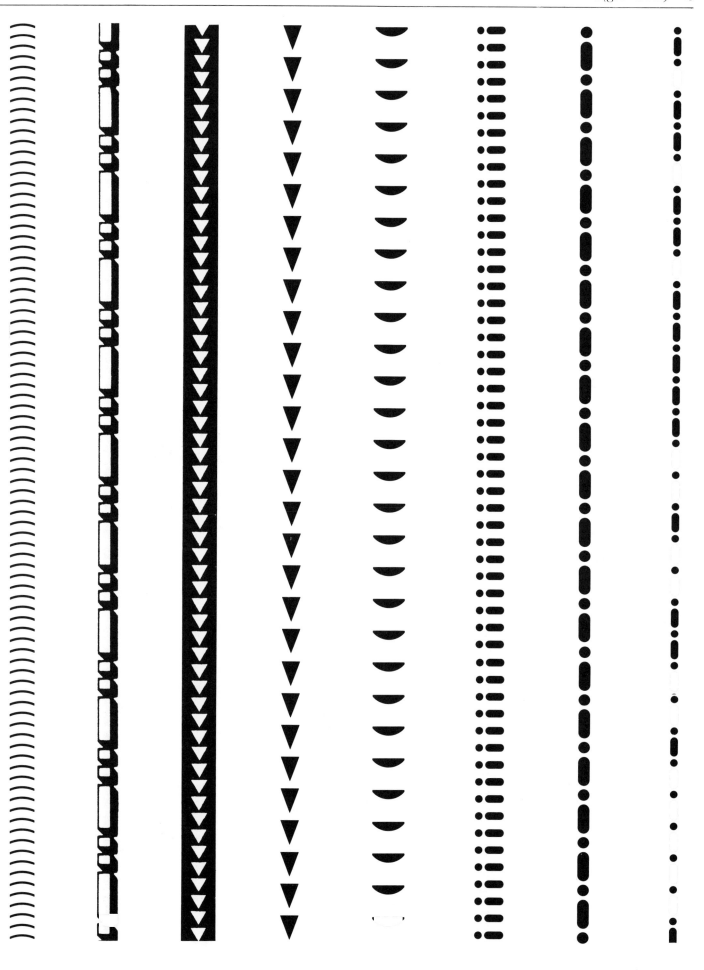

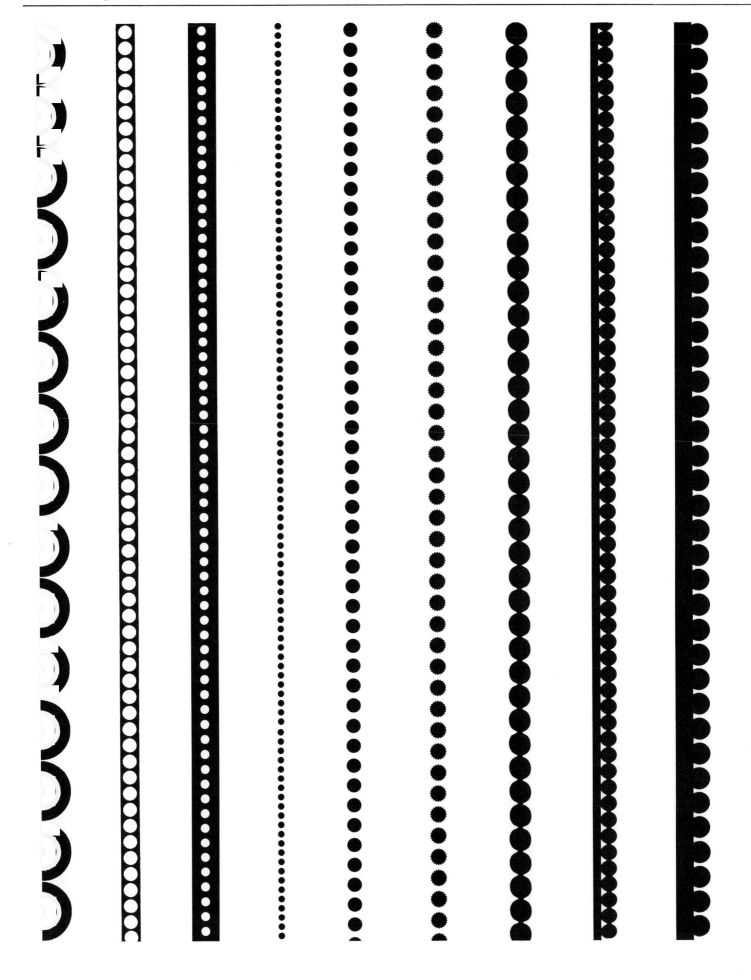

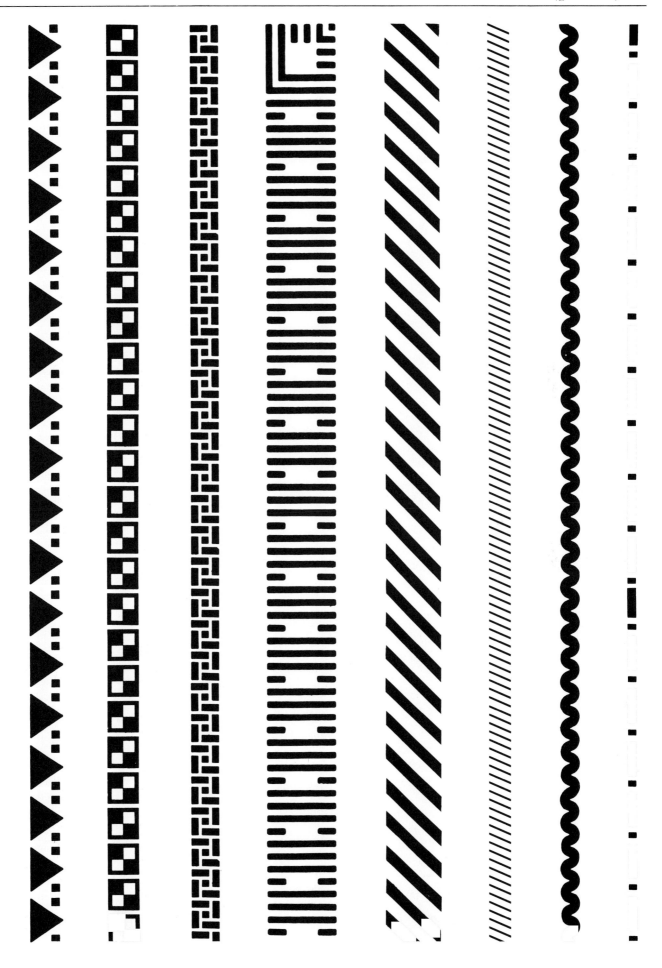

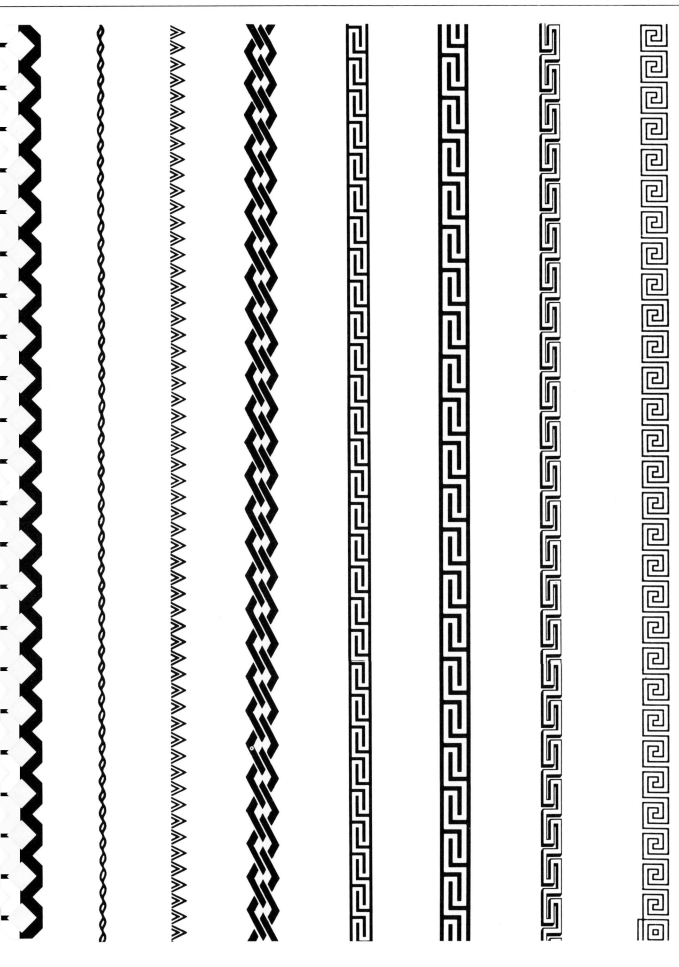

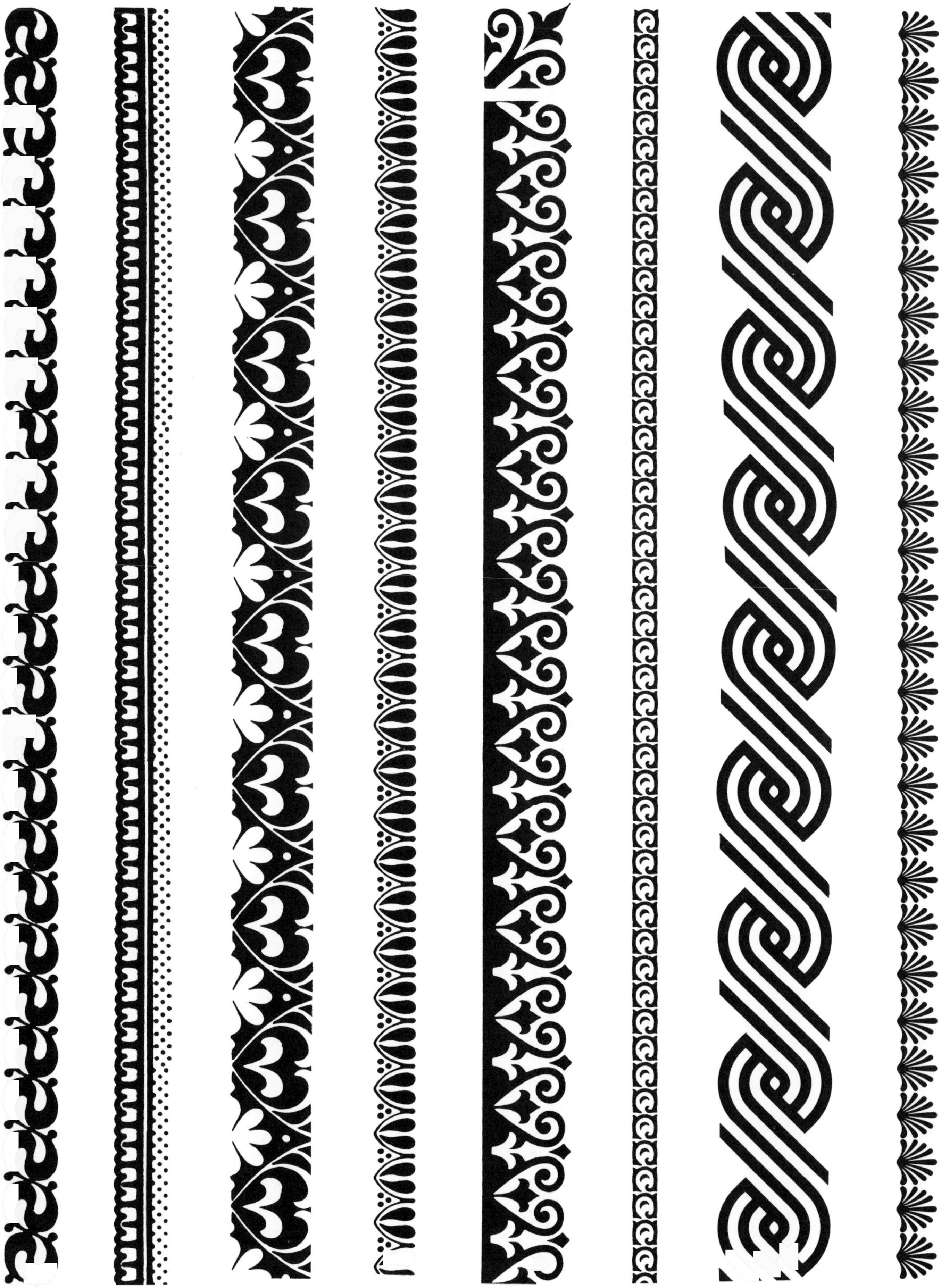

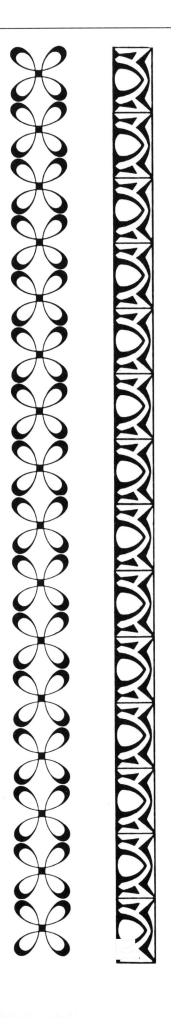

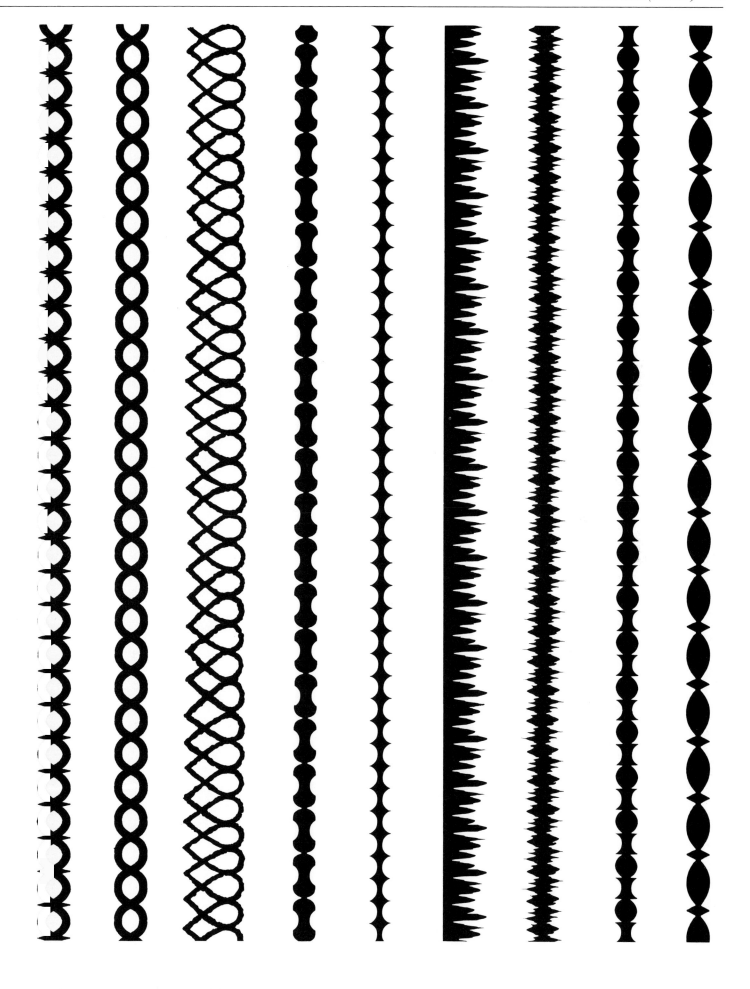

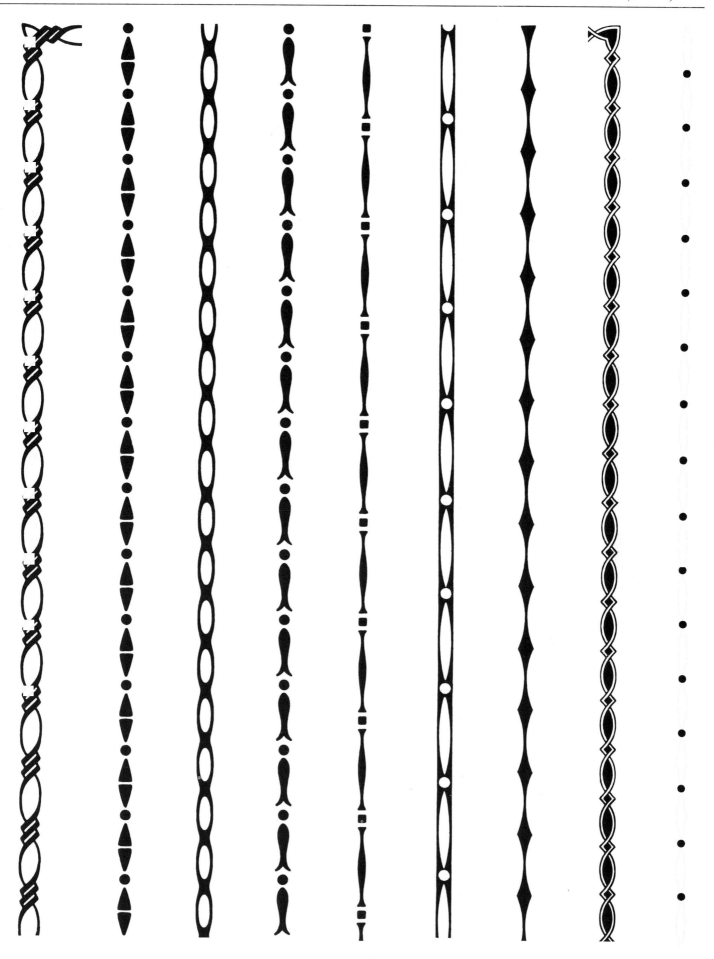

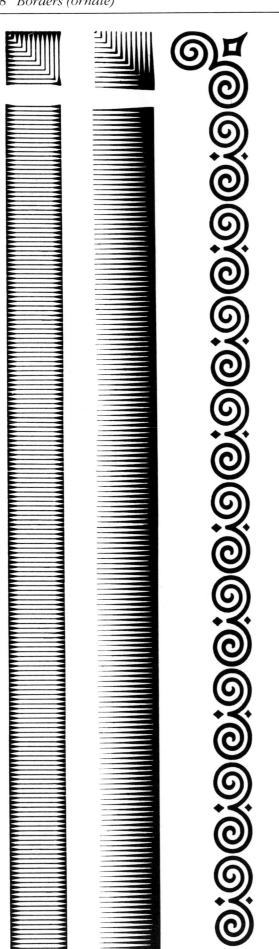

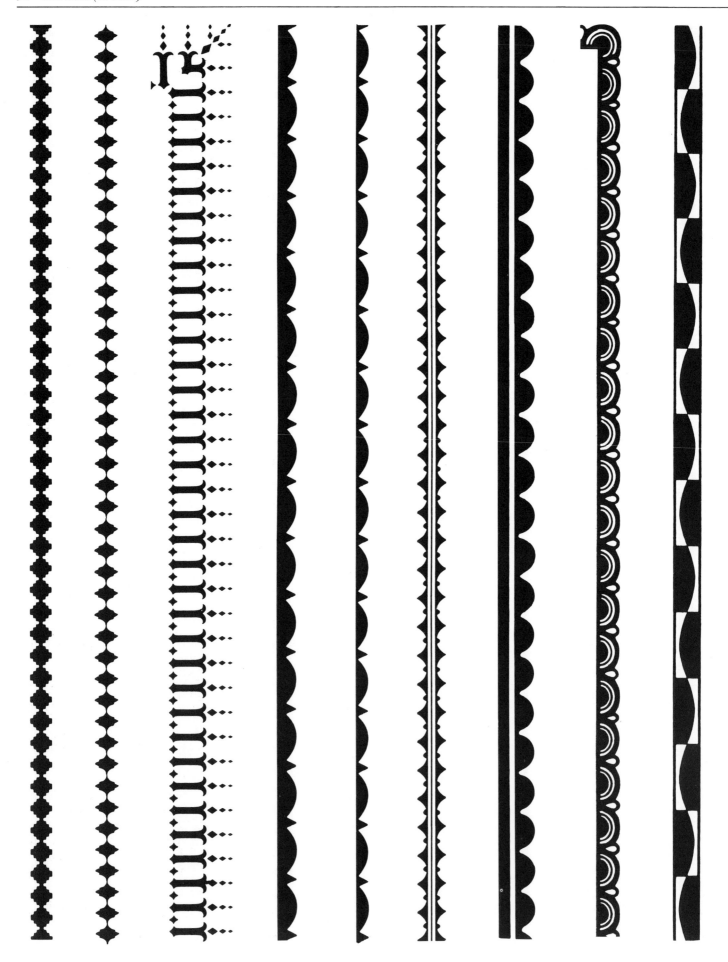

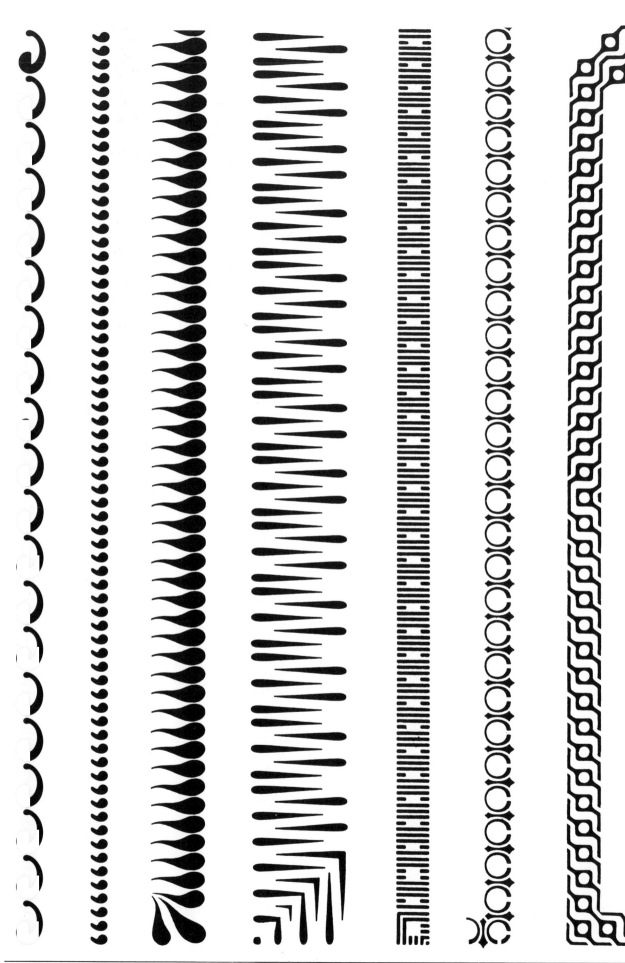

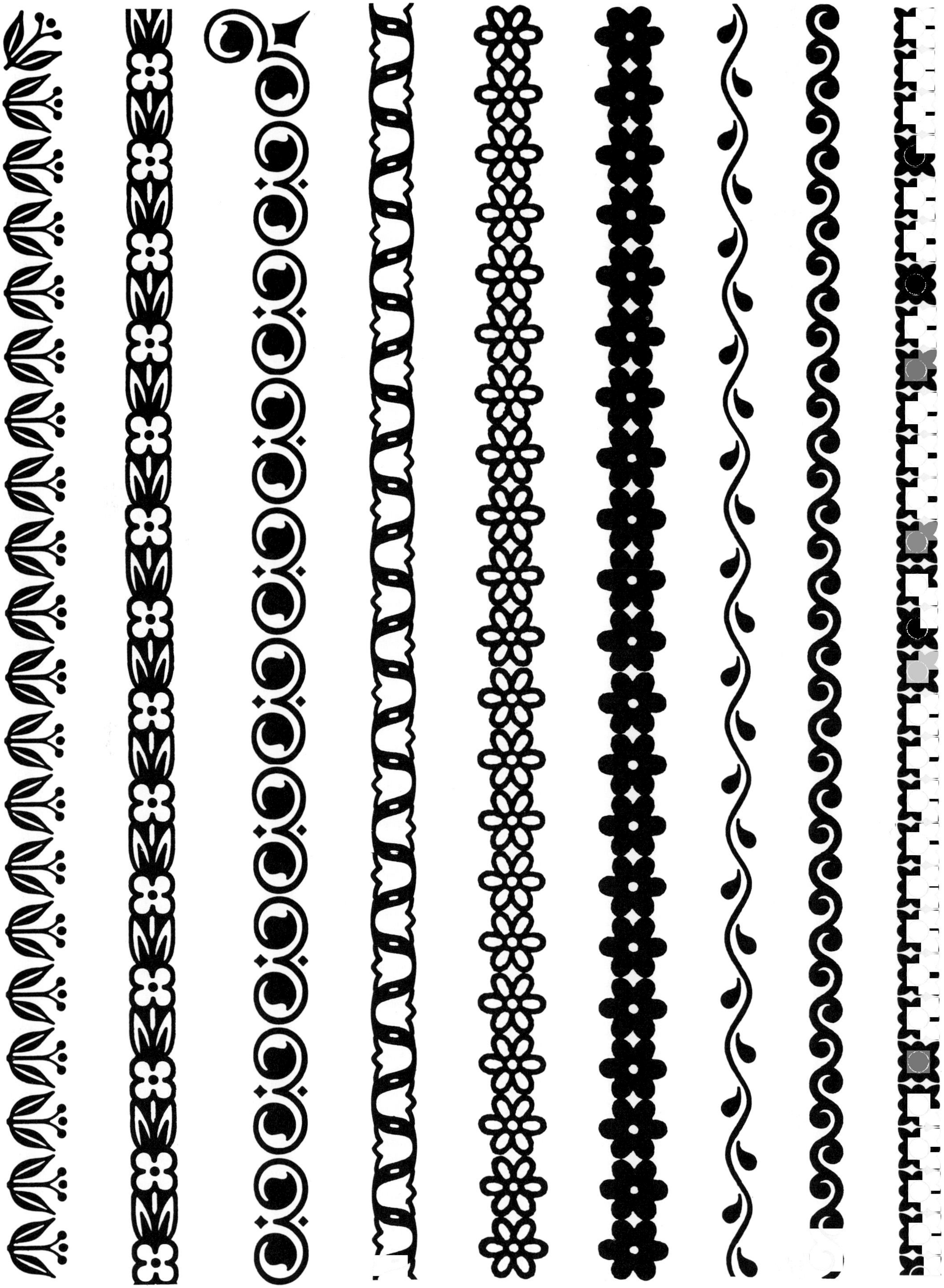

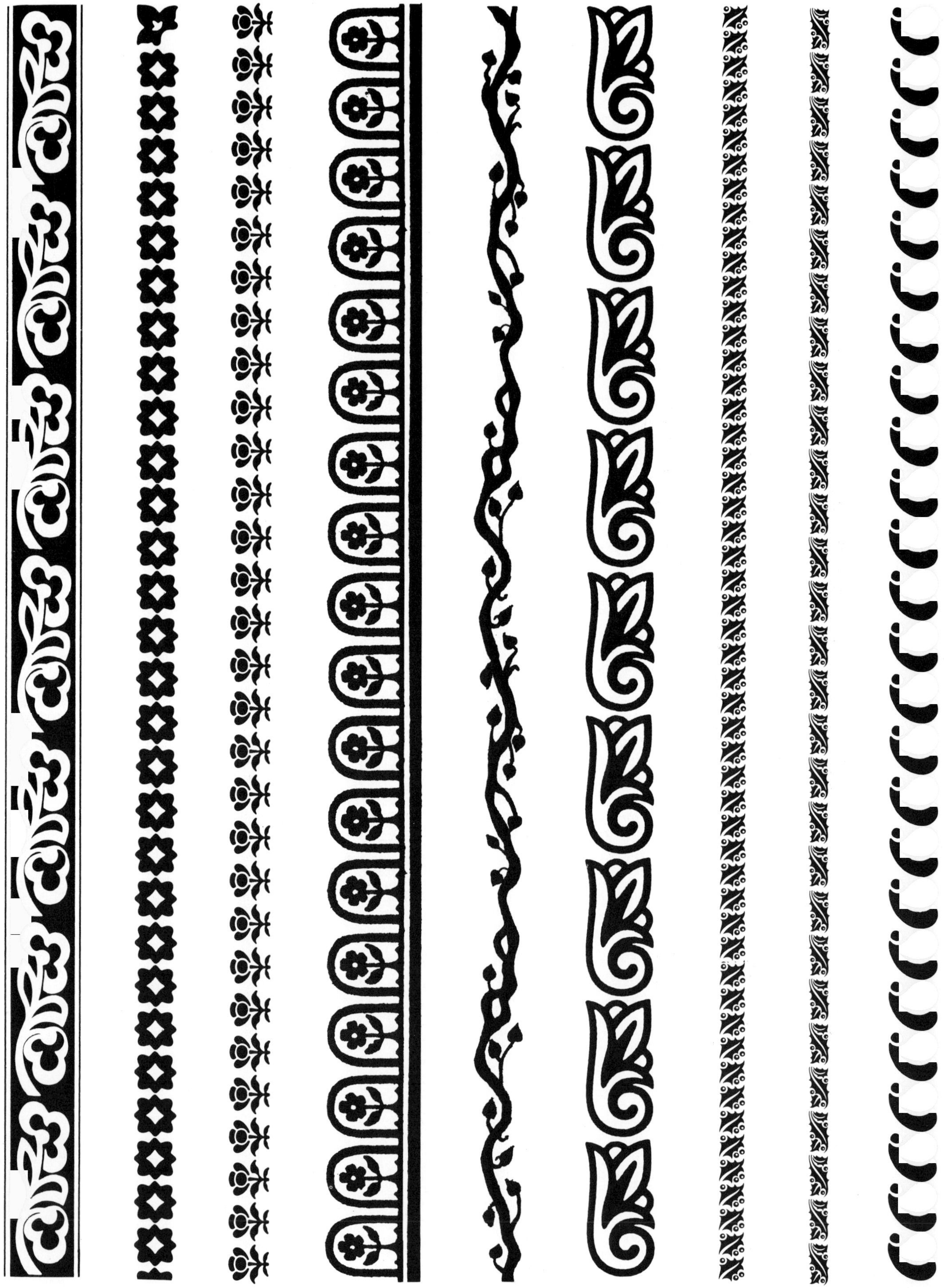

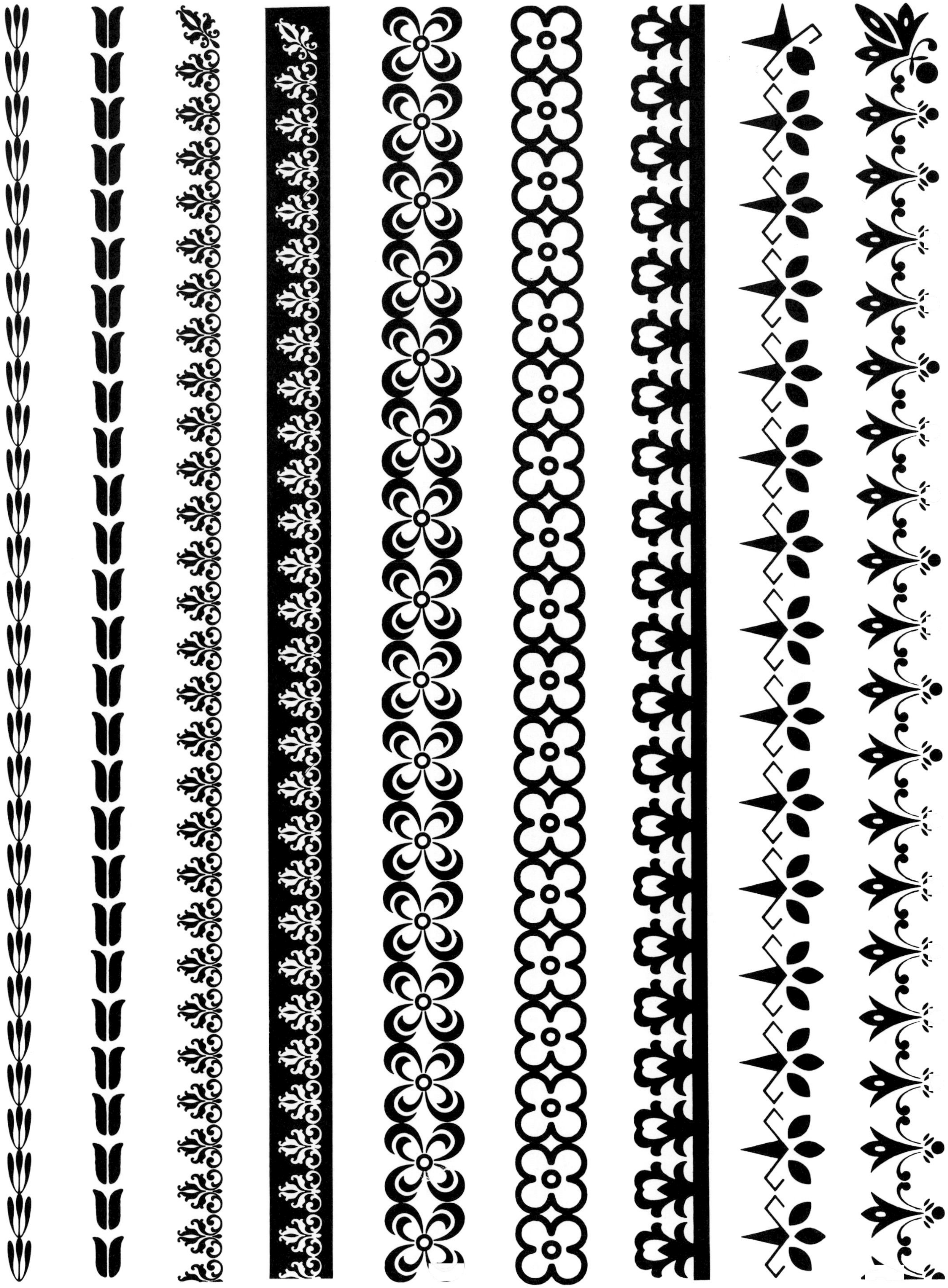

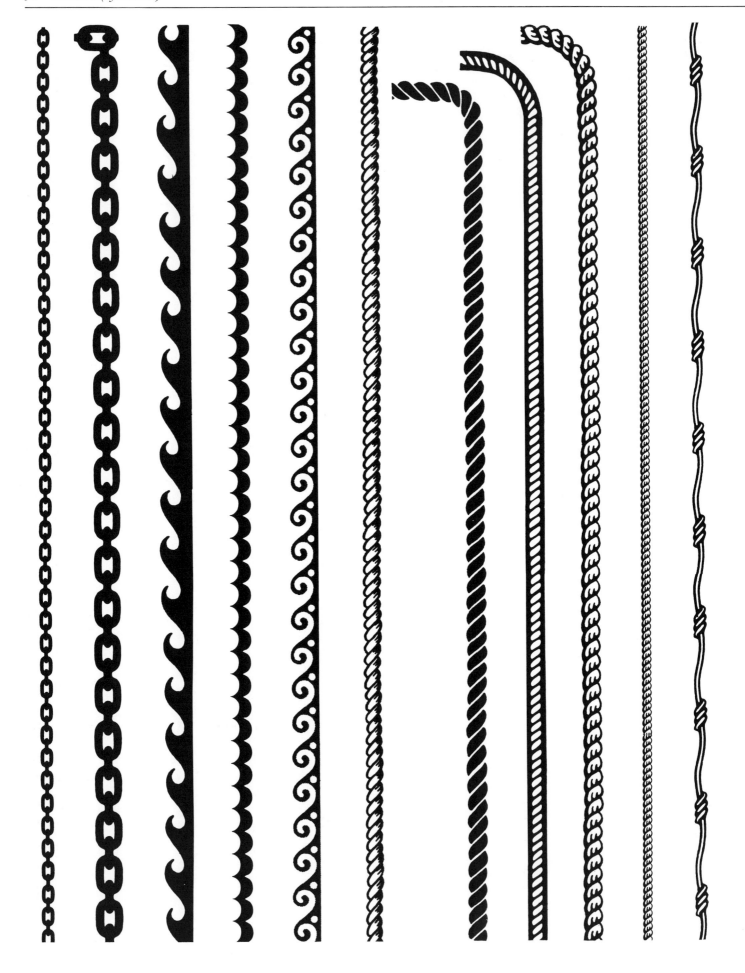

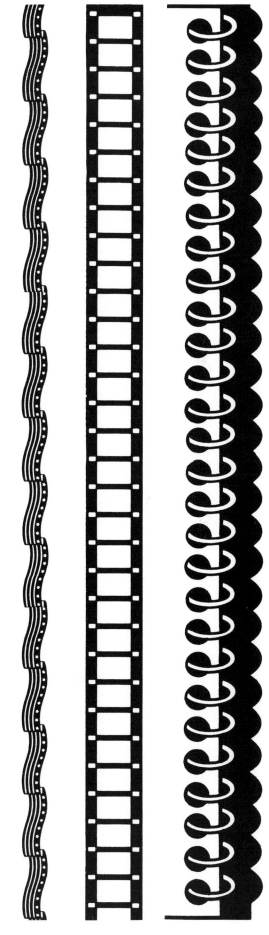

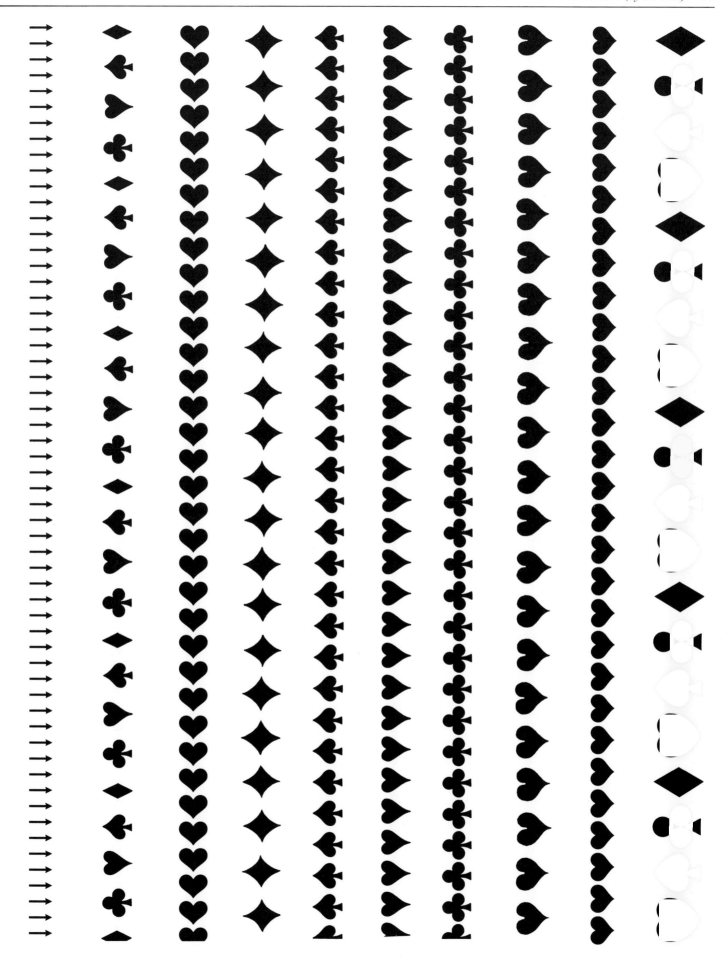

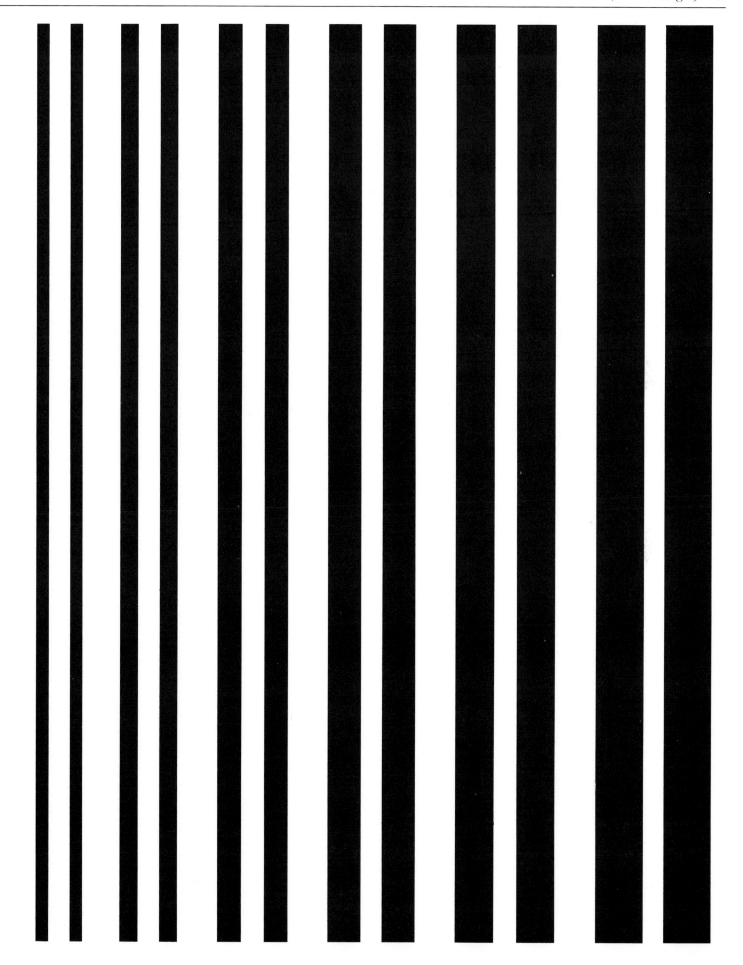

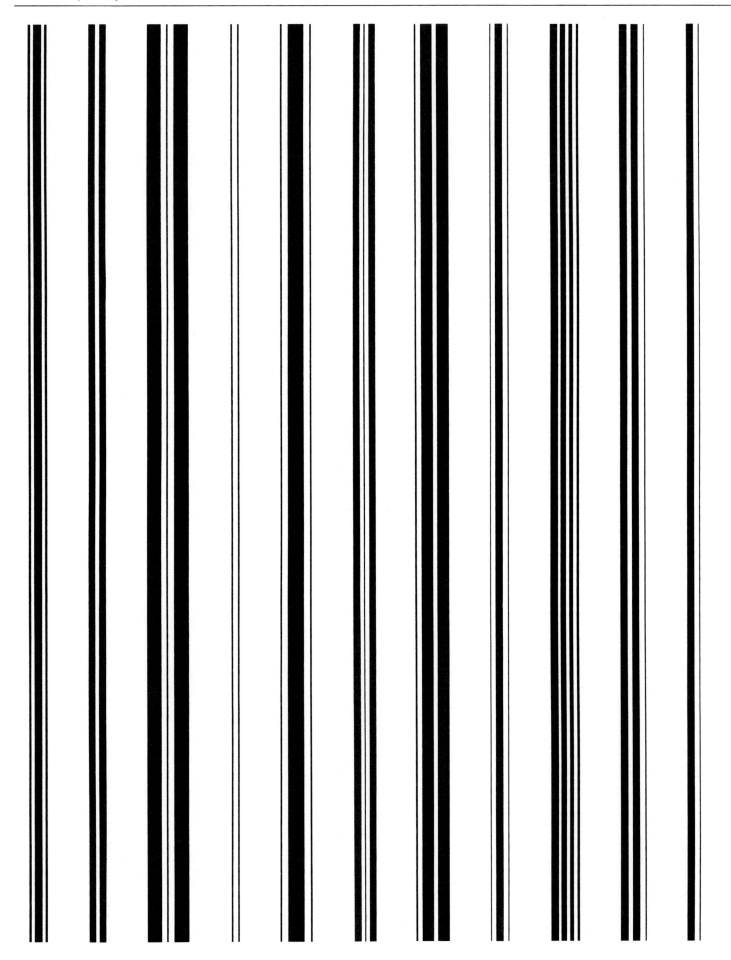

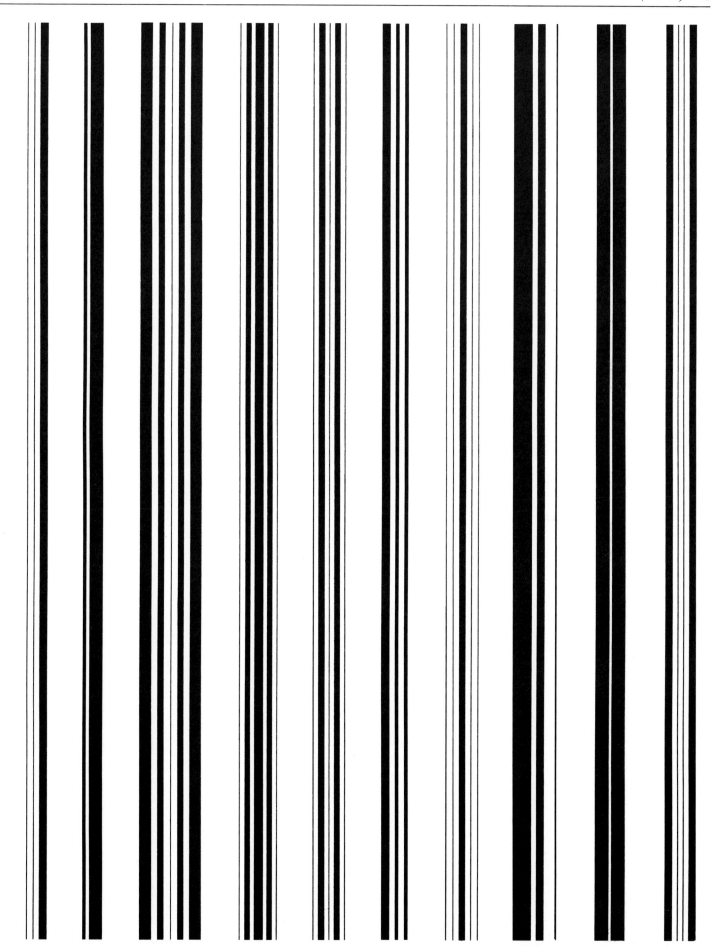

Corners (ornate)
Corners (art nouveau)
Corners (geometric)
Cornices

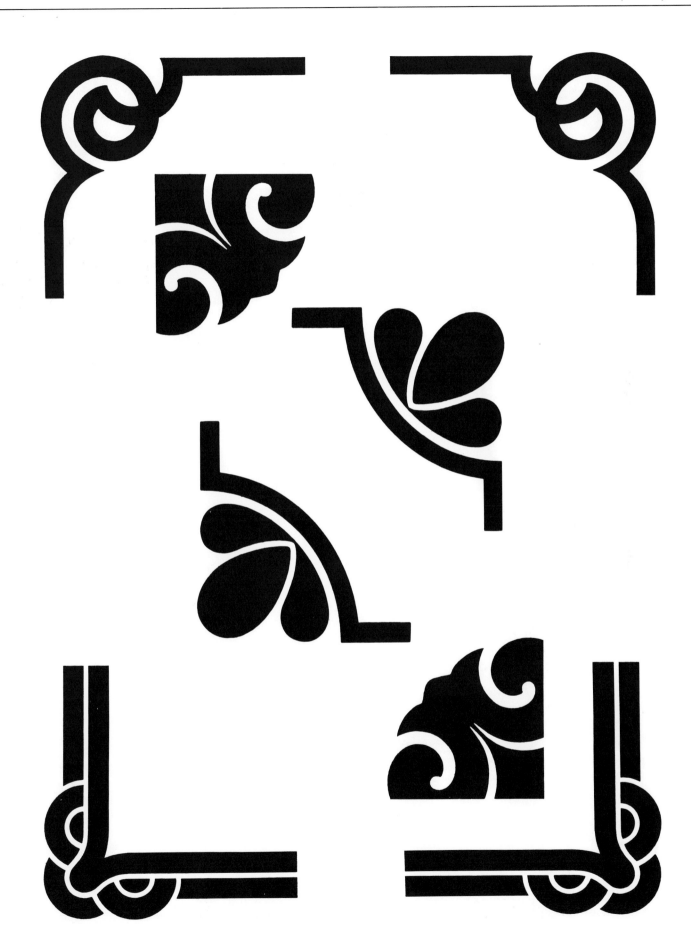

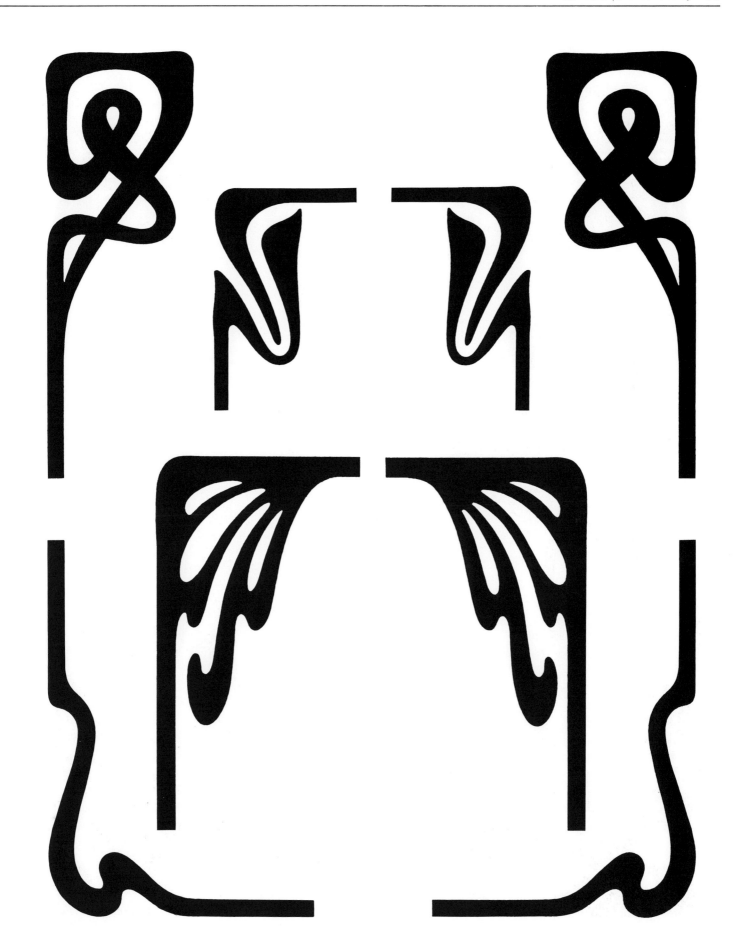

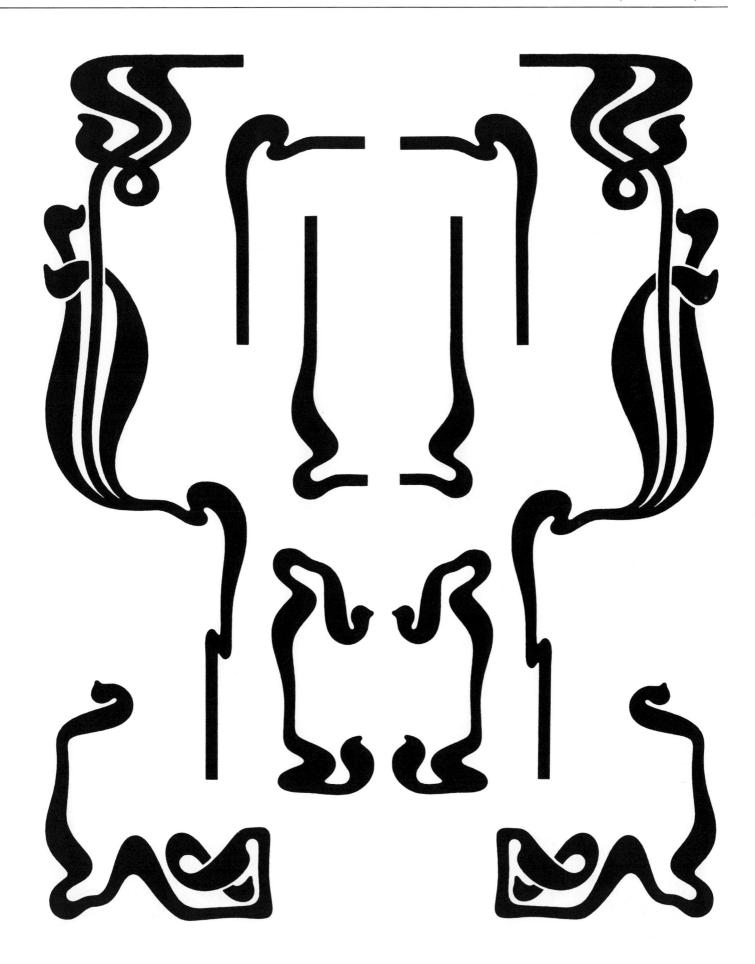

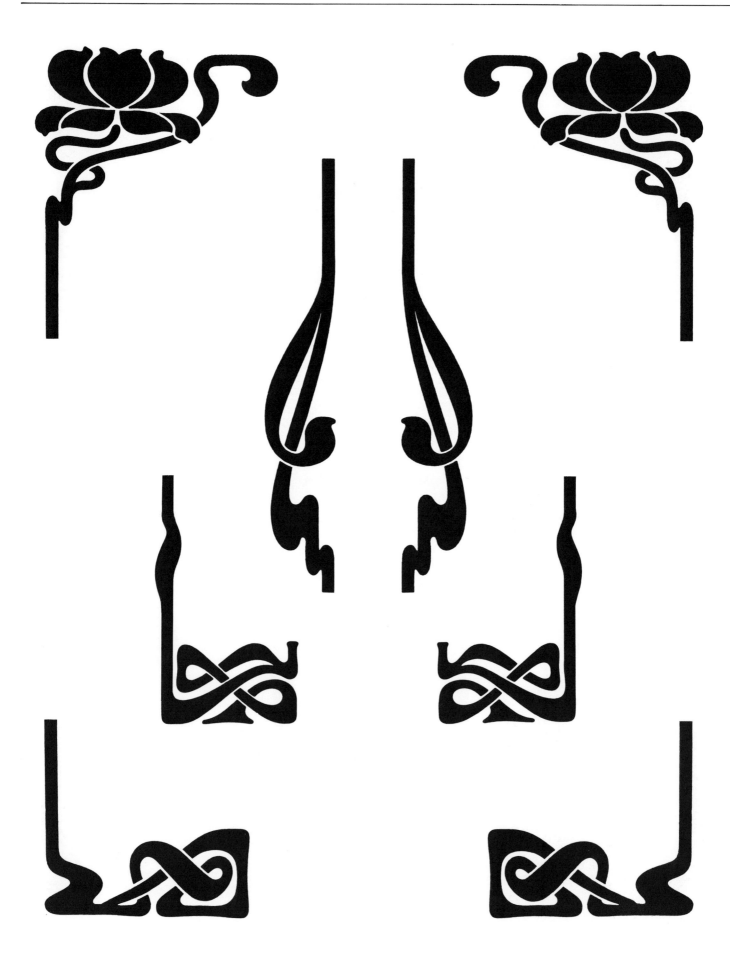

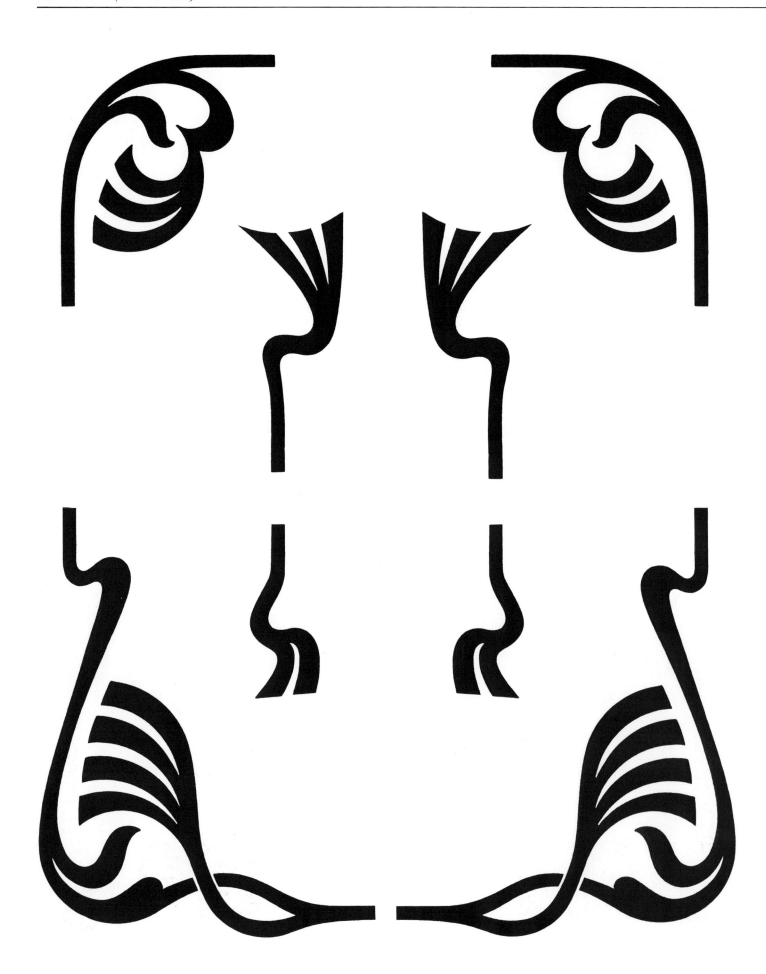

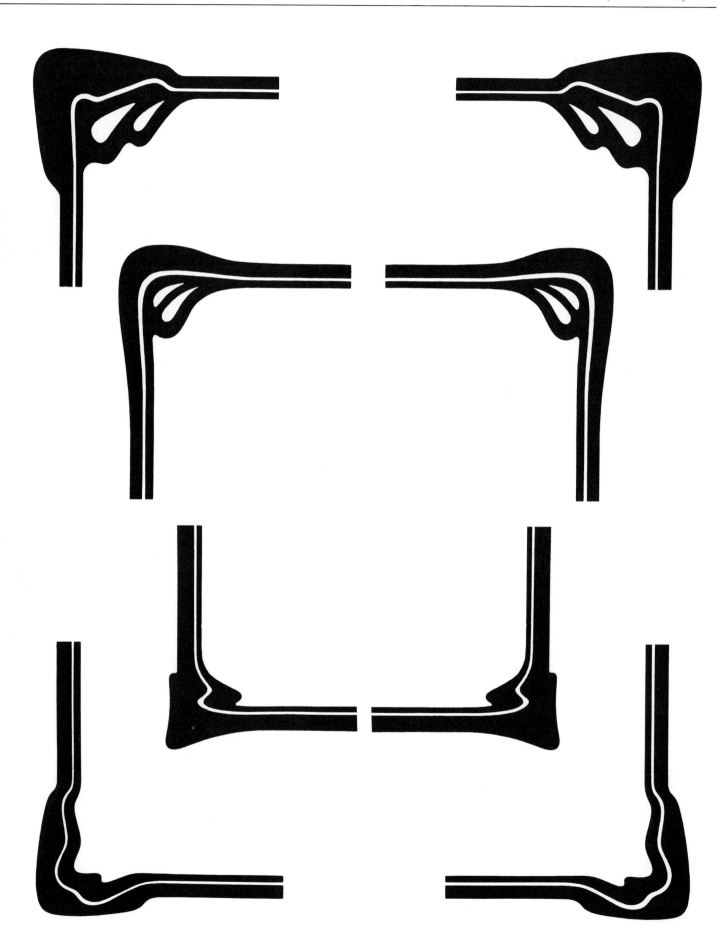

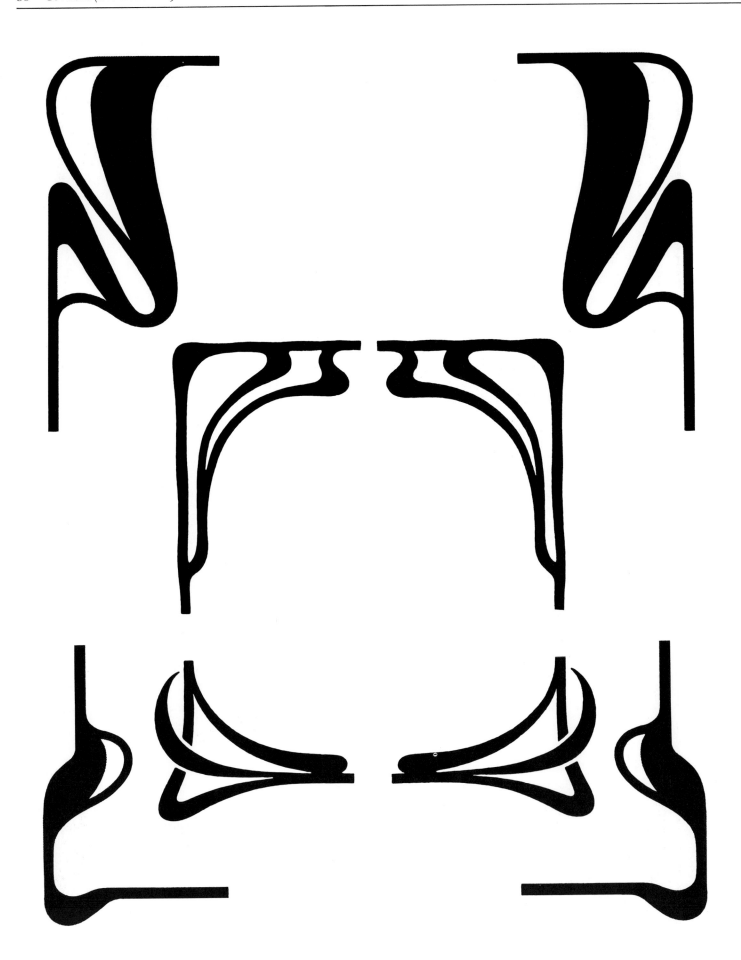

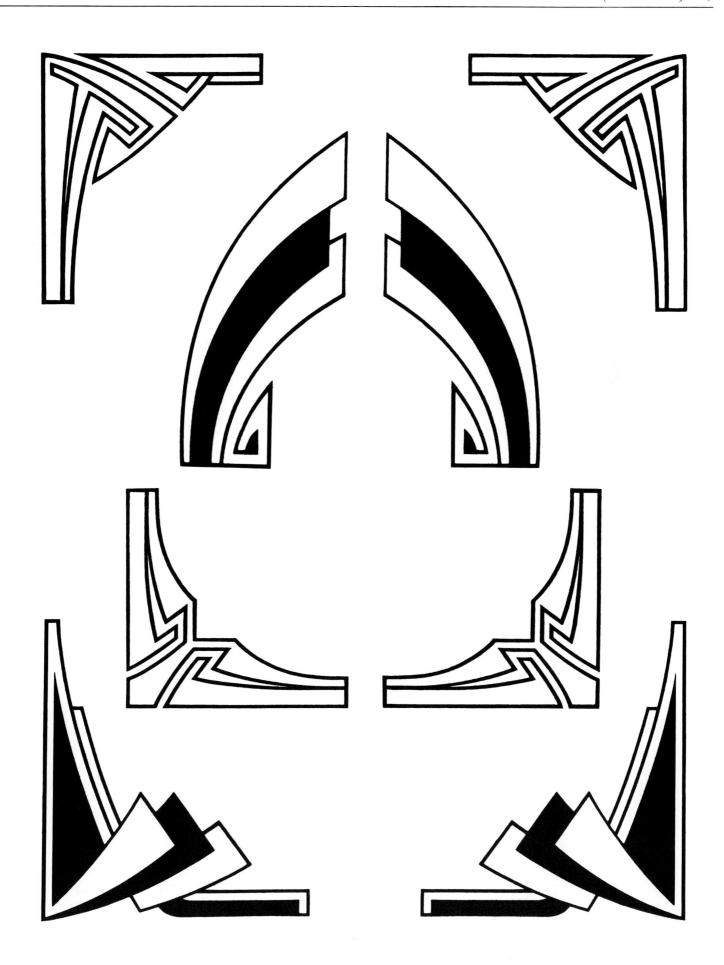

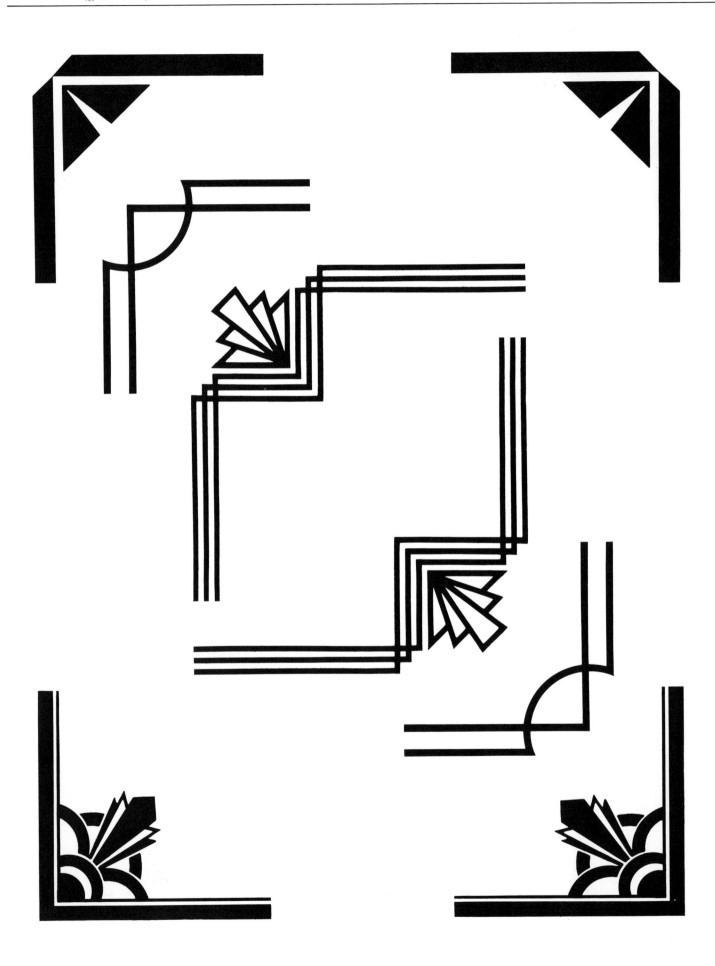

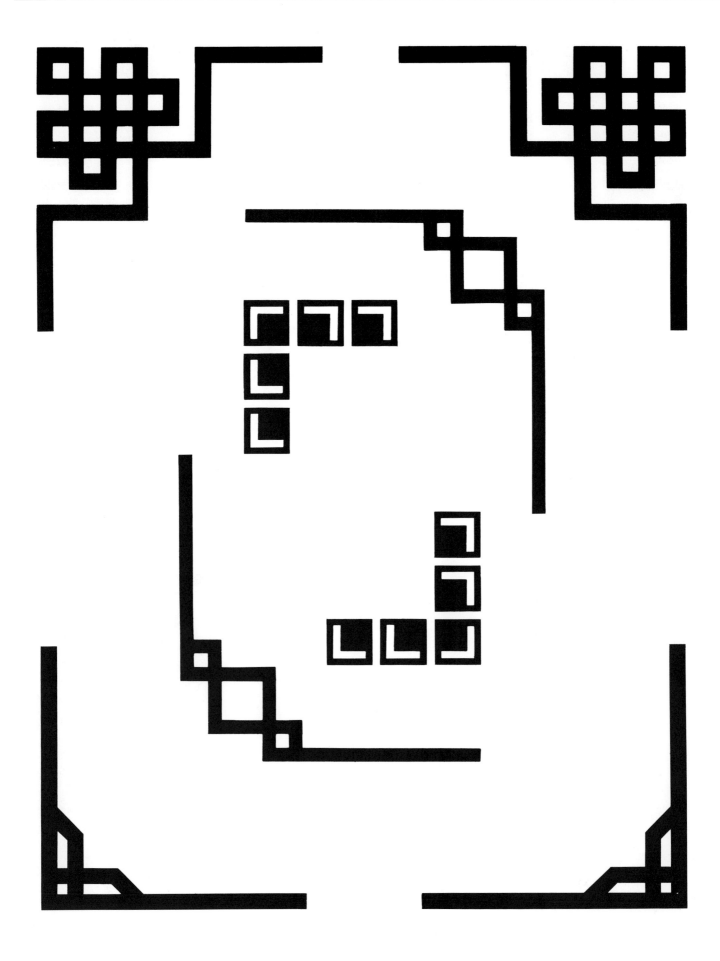

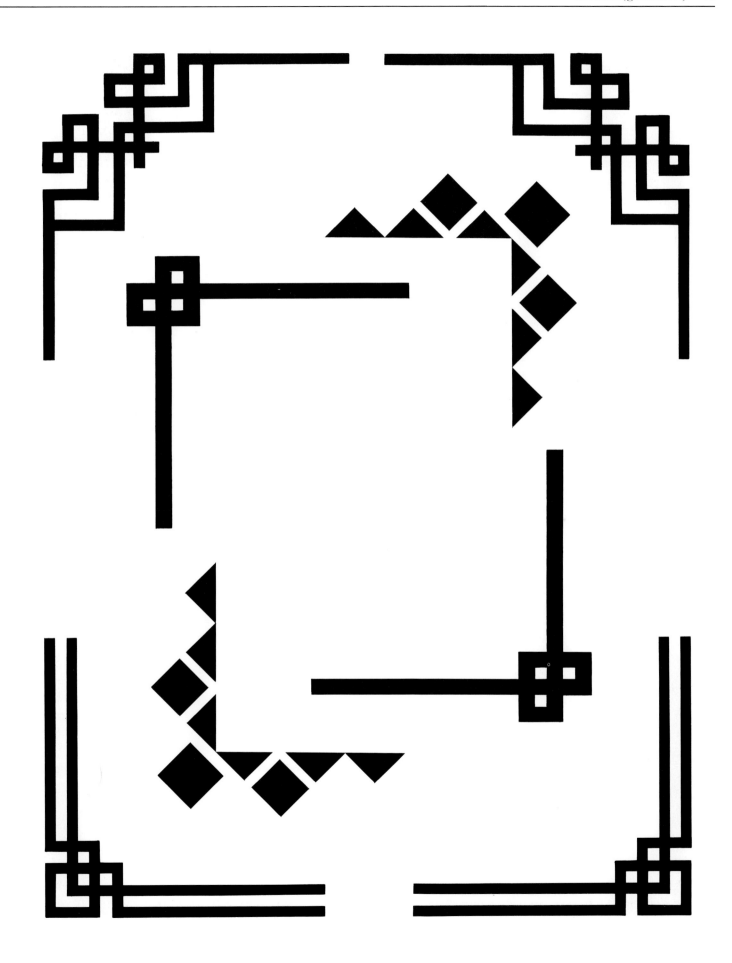

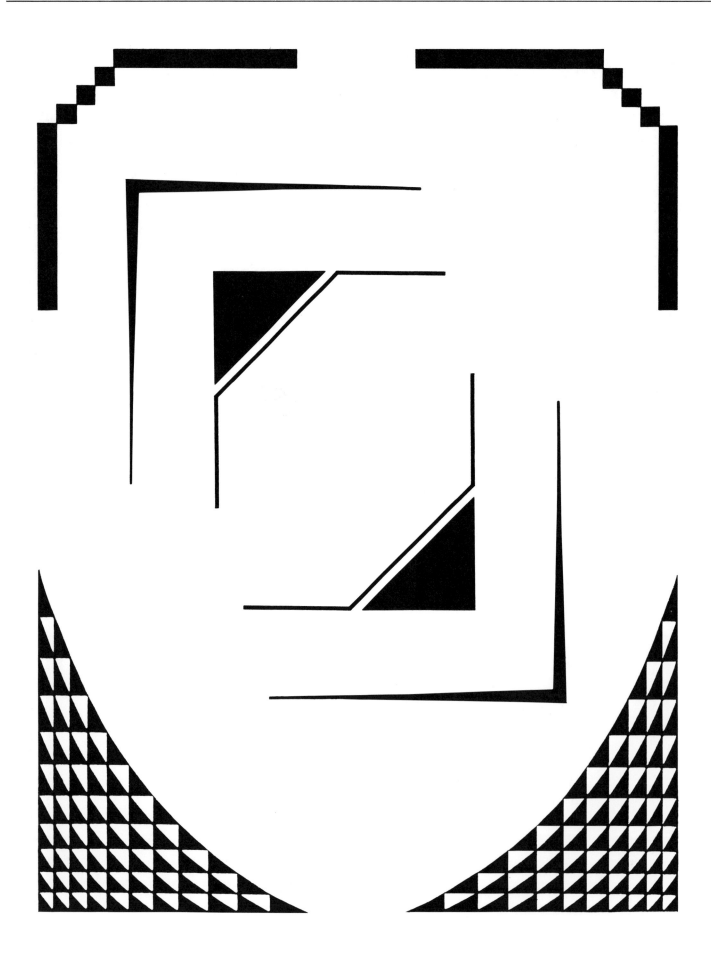

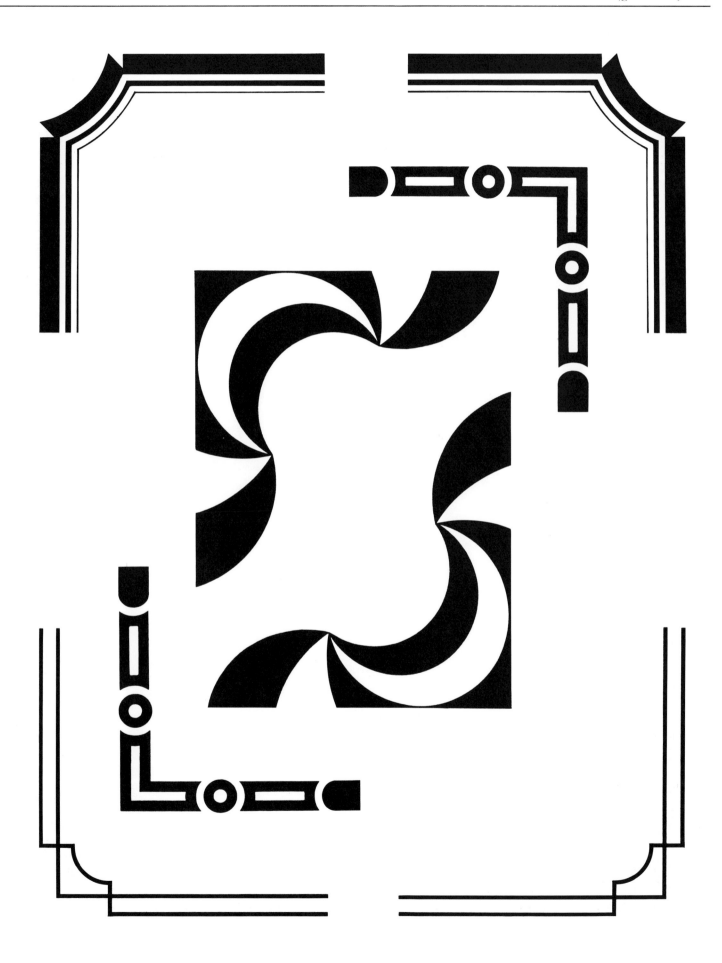

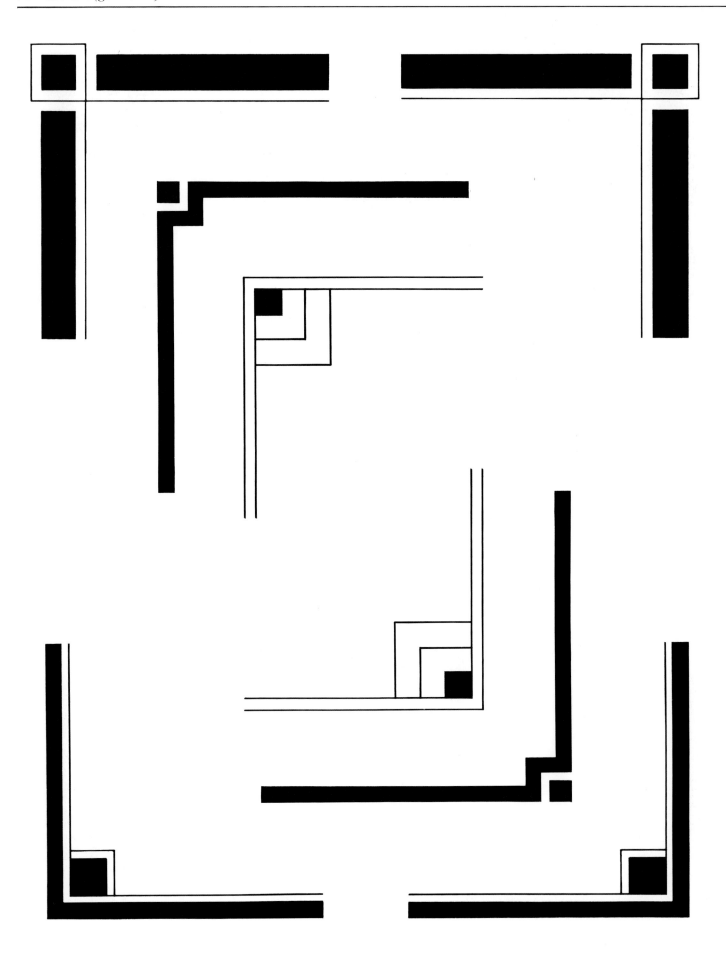

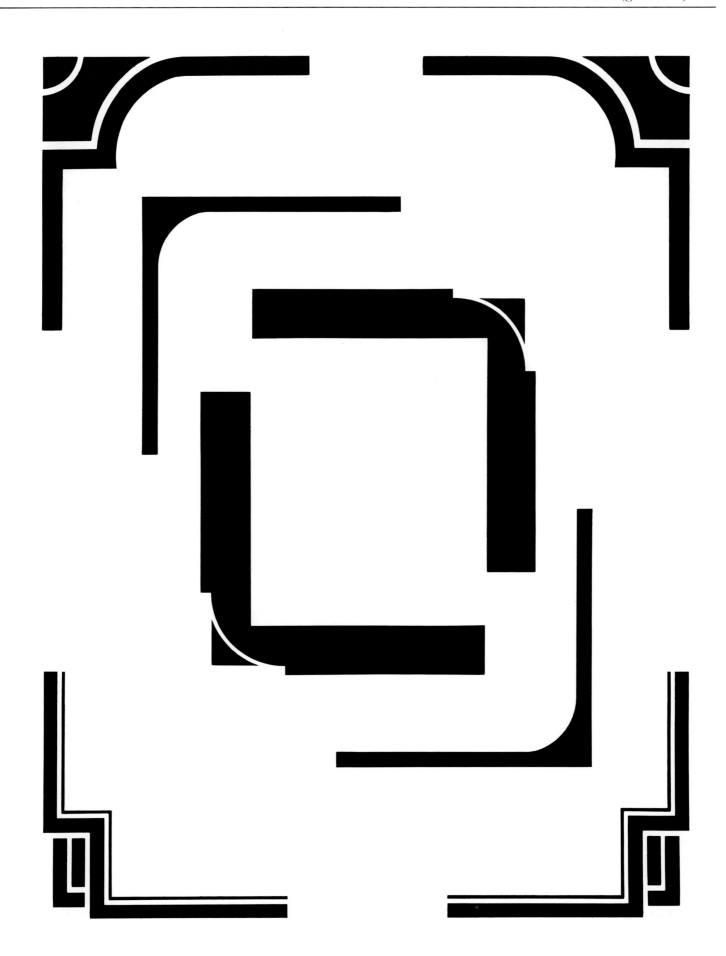

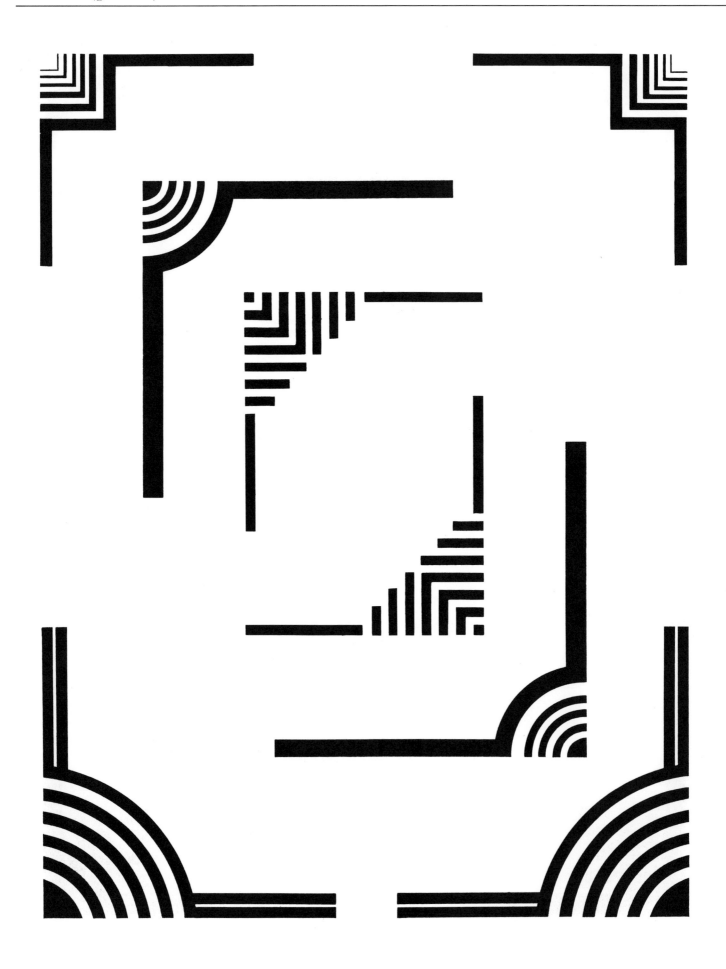

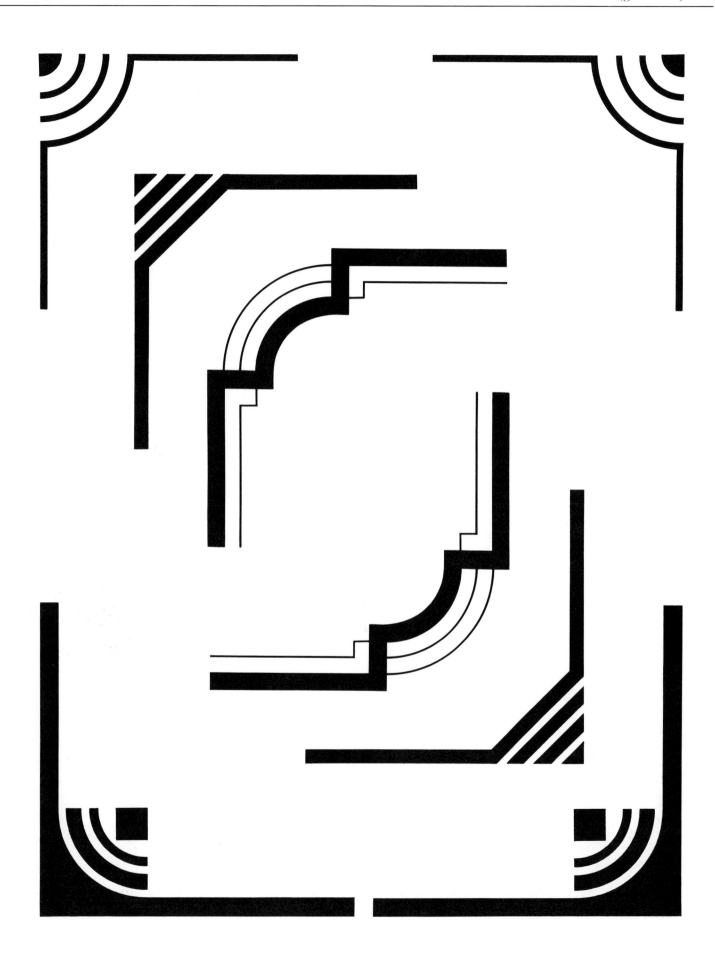

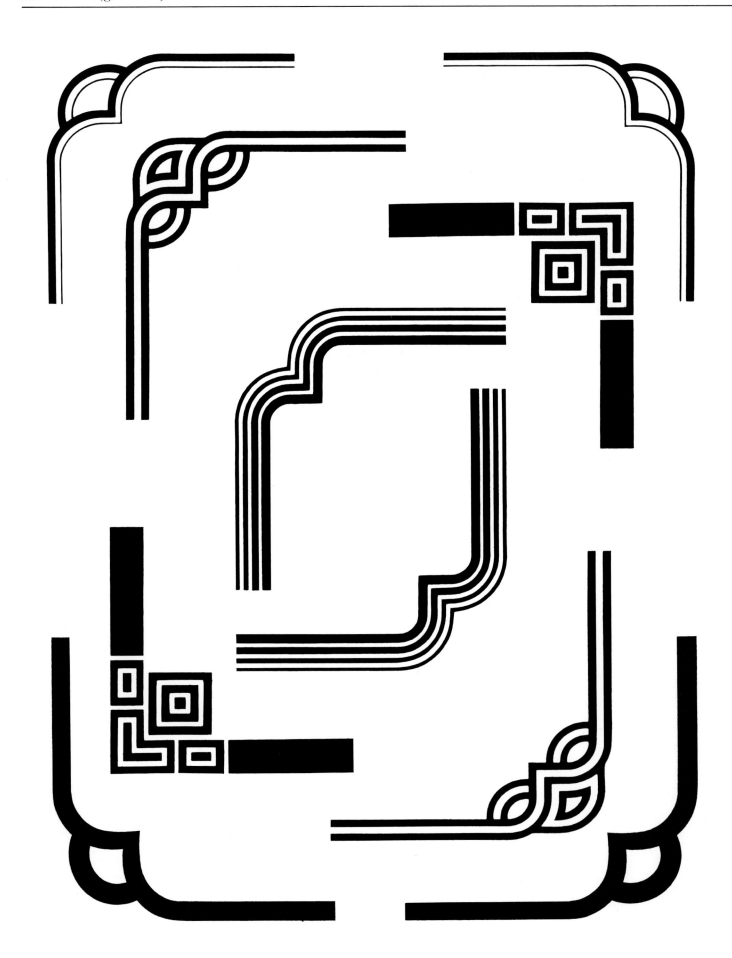

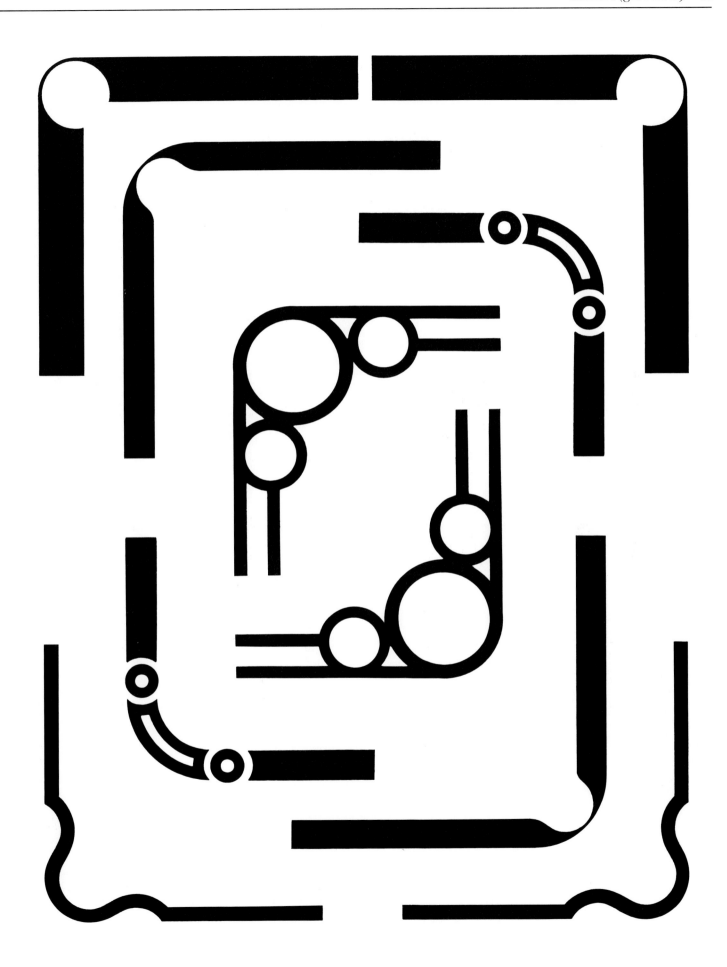

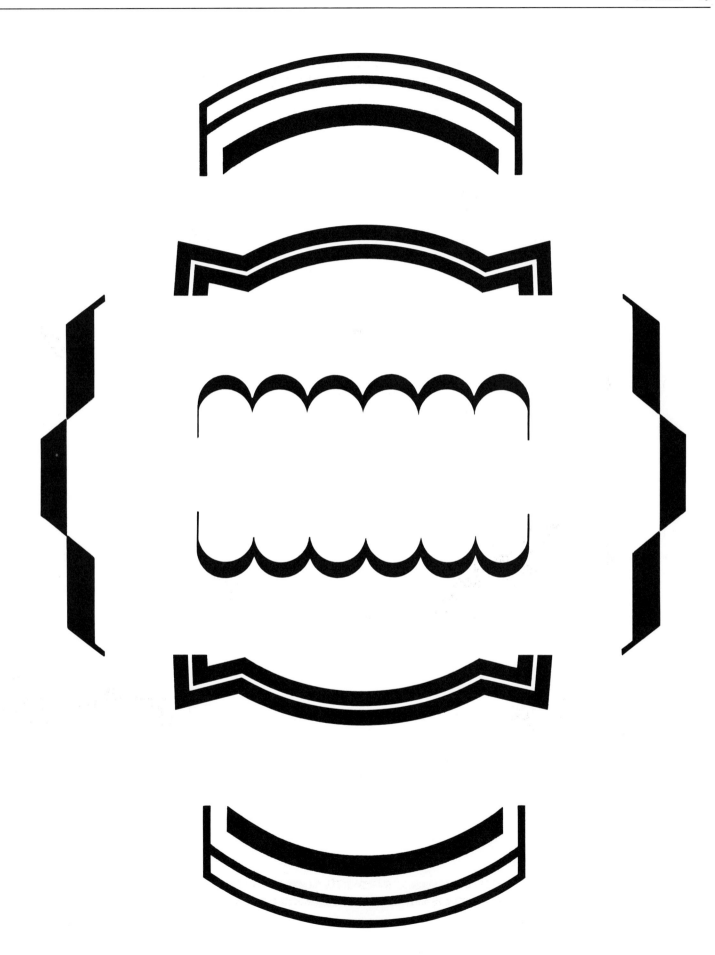

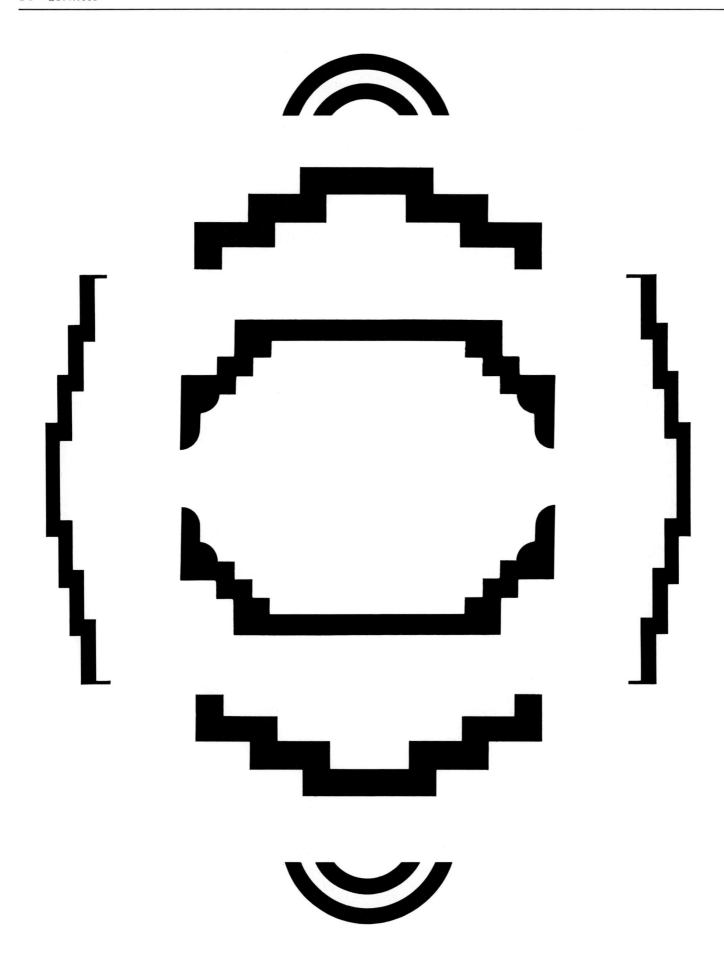

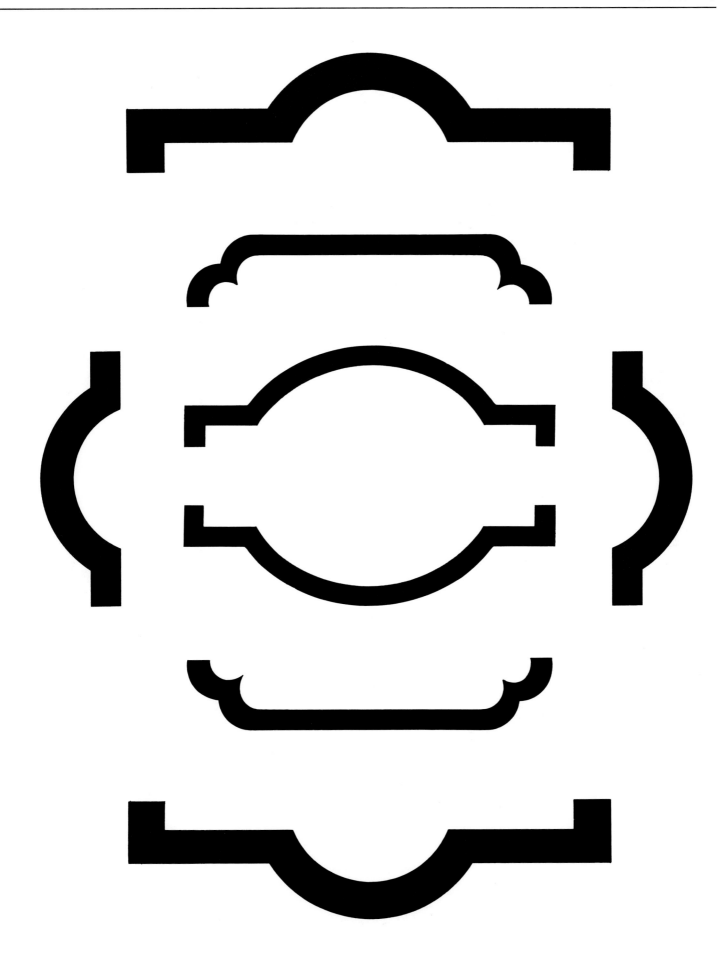

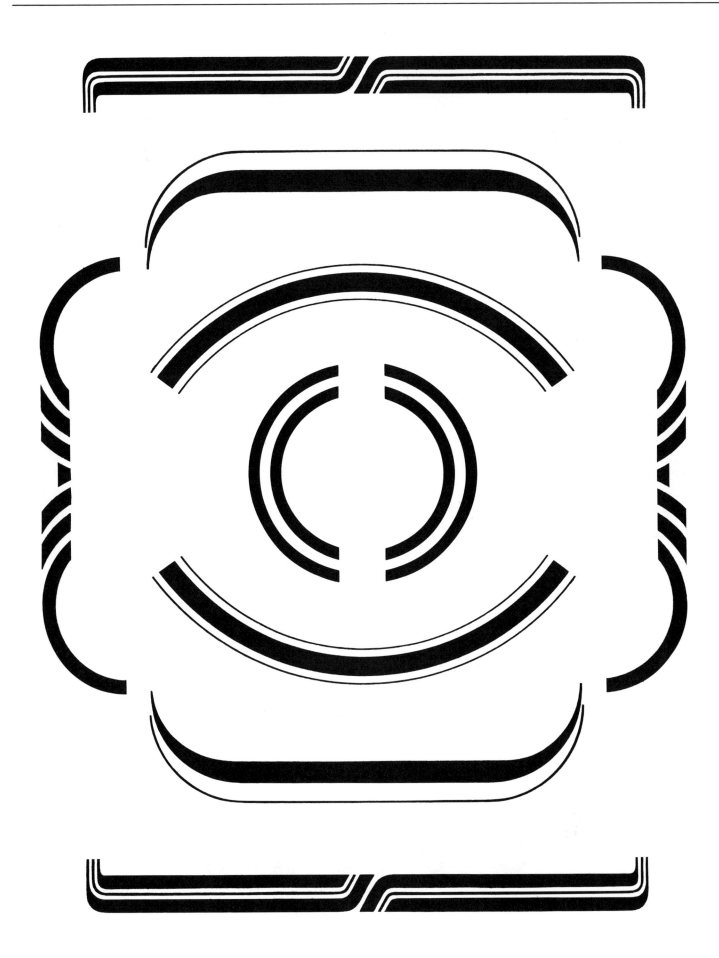

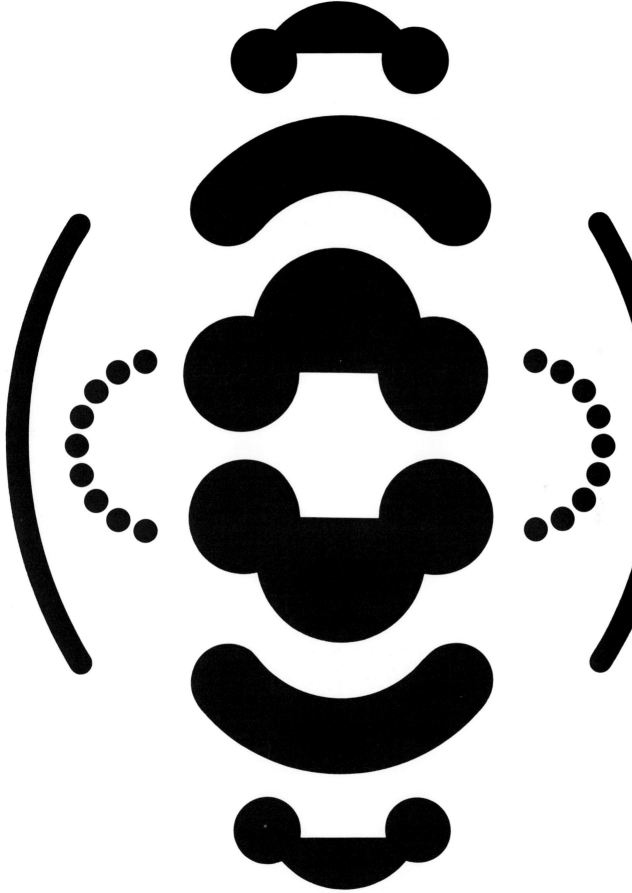

Brackets/Braces
Brackets (decorative)
Dashes/Whiskers
Printer's Ornaments
Printer's Ornaments
(fleur de lis)
Printer's Ornaments
(art nouveau)

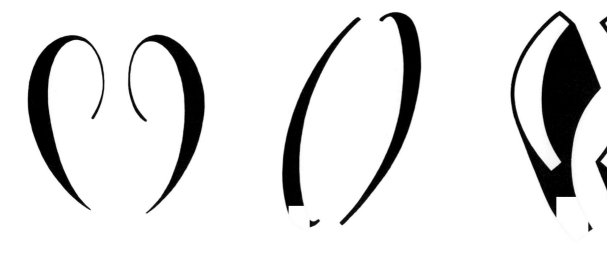

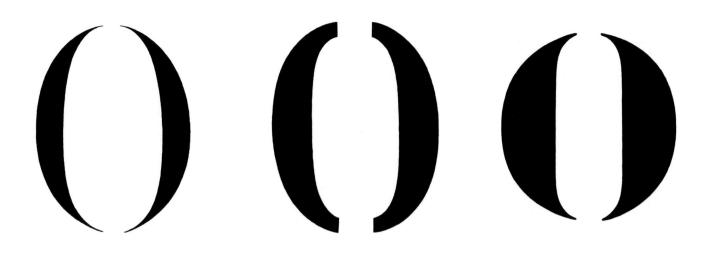

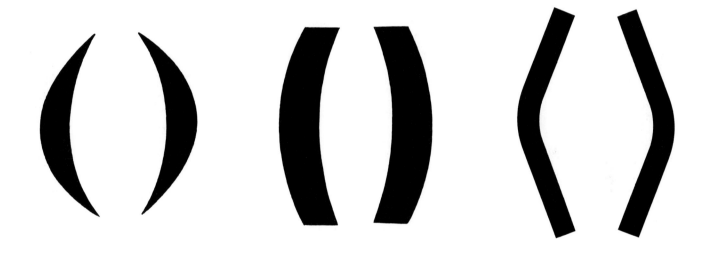

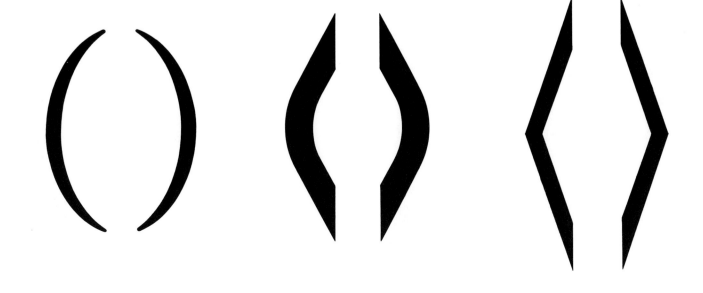

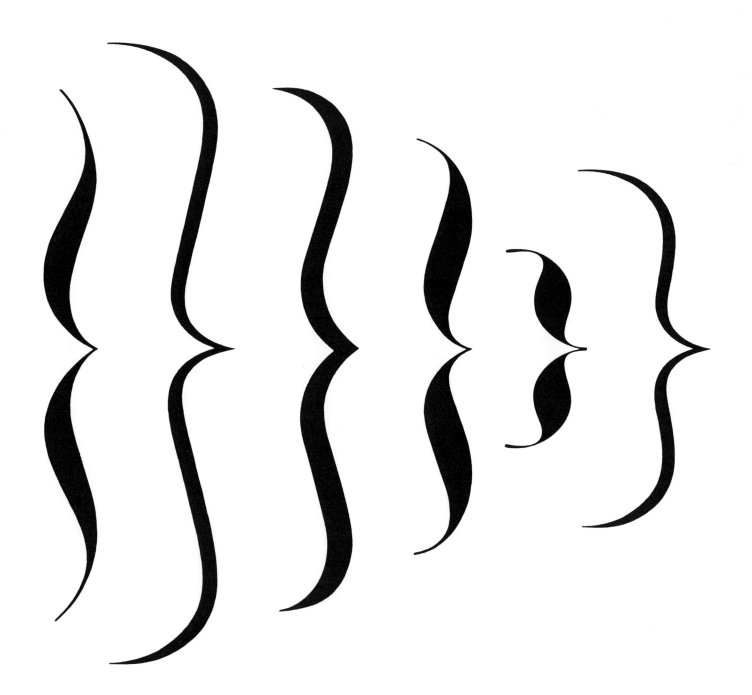

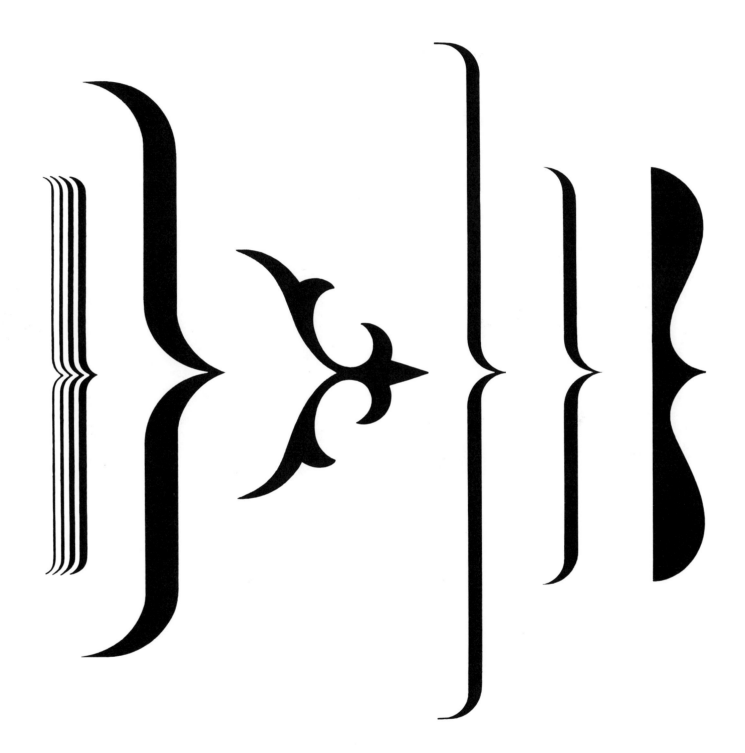

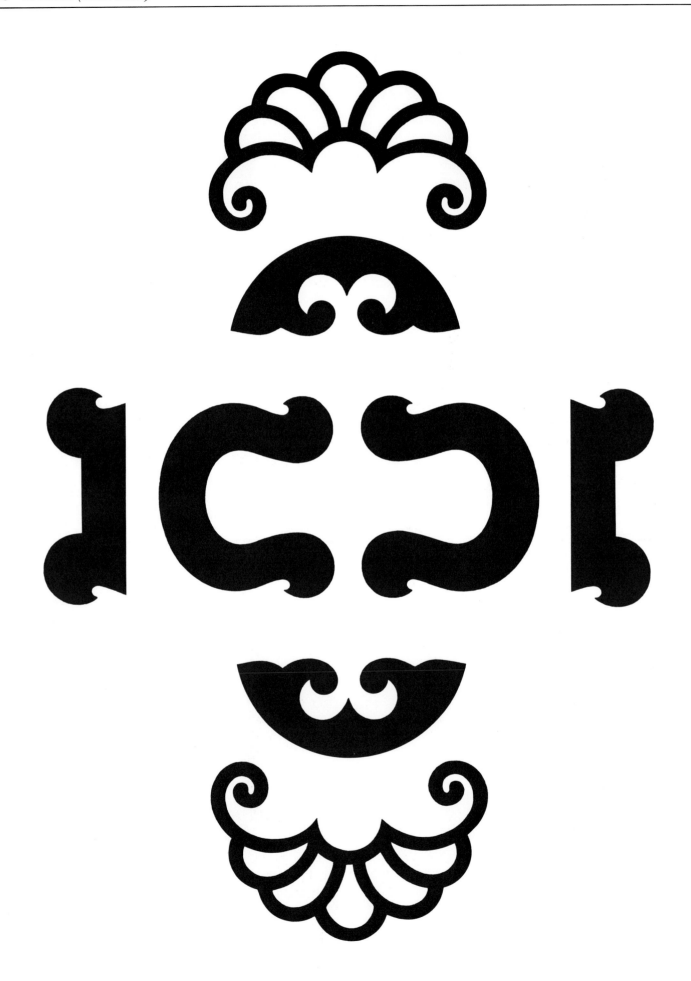

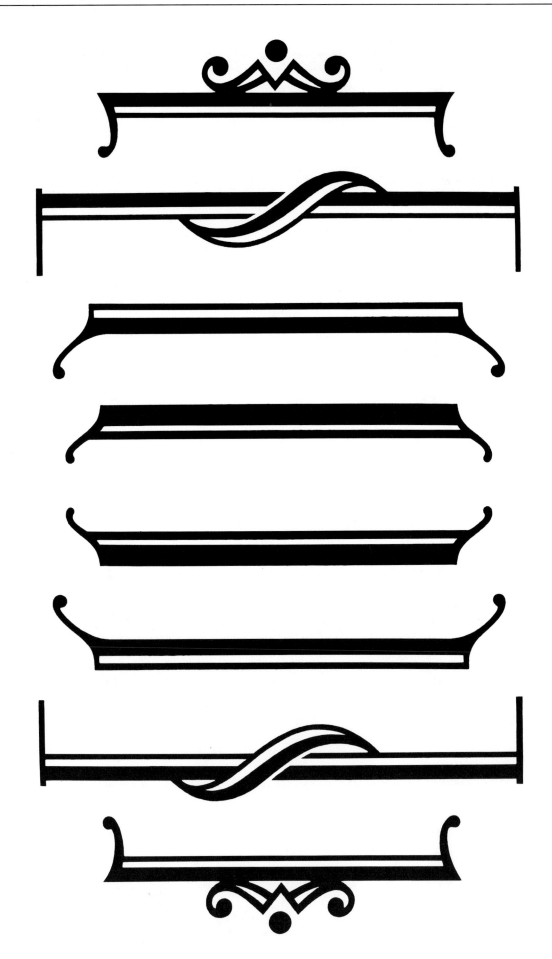

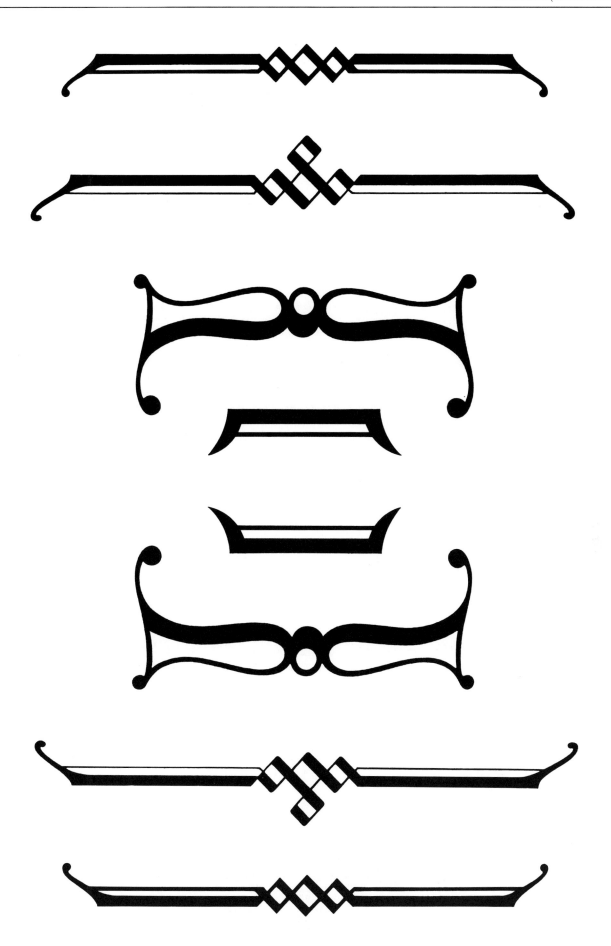

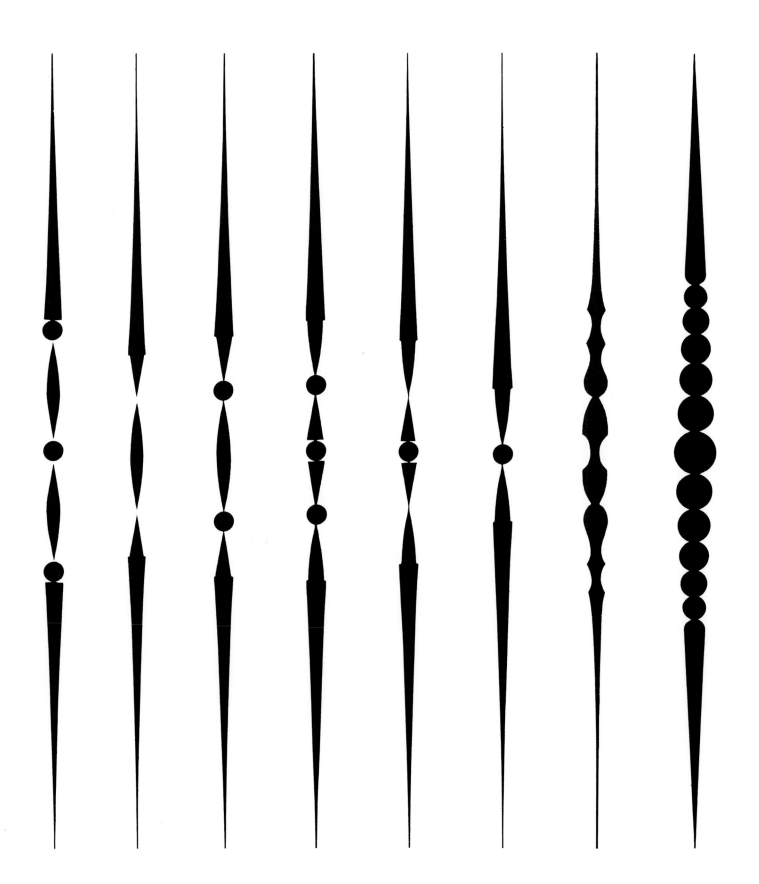

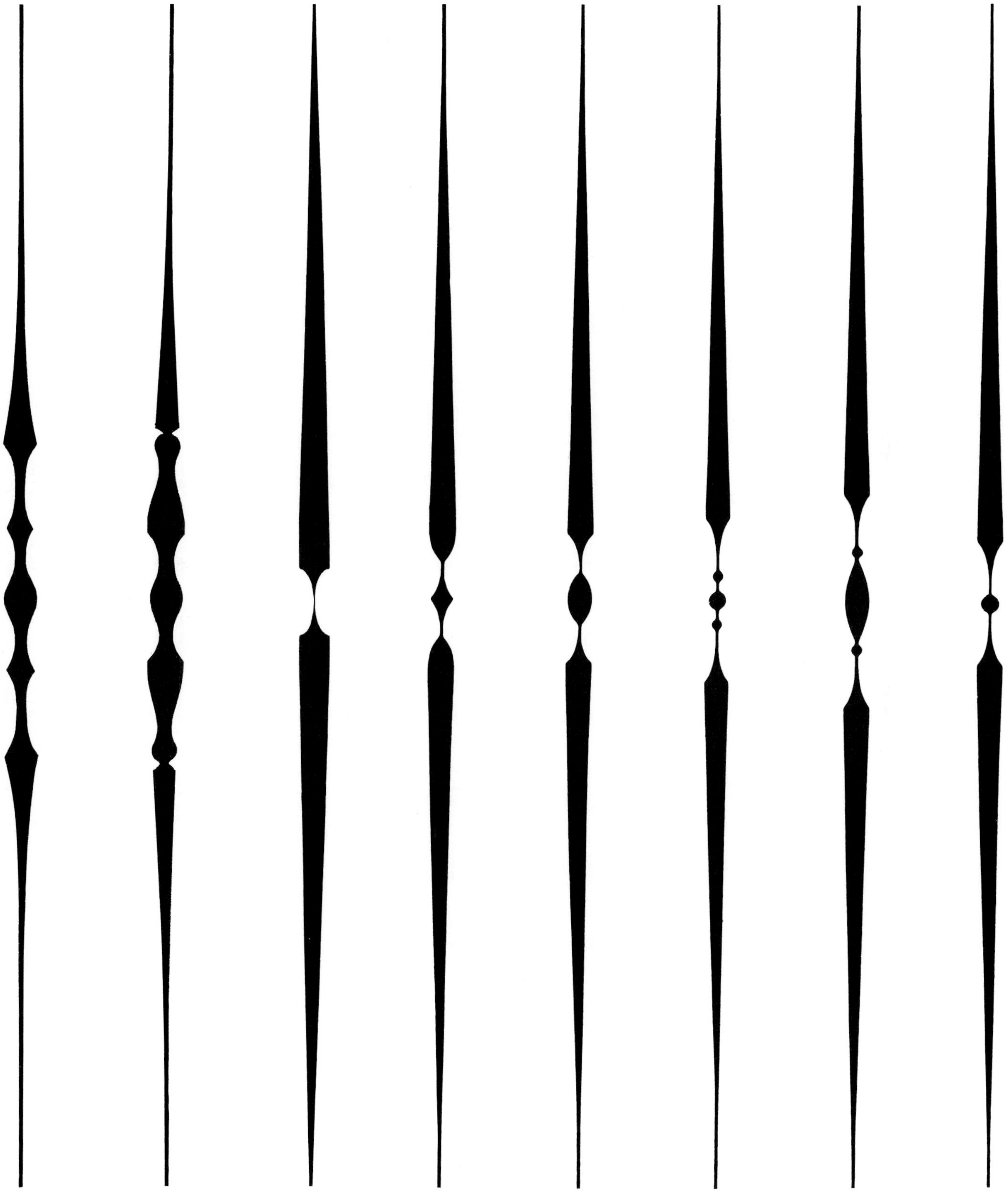

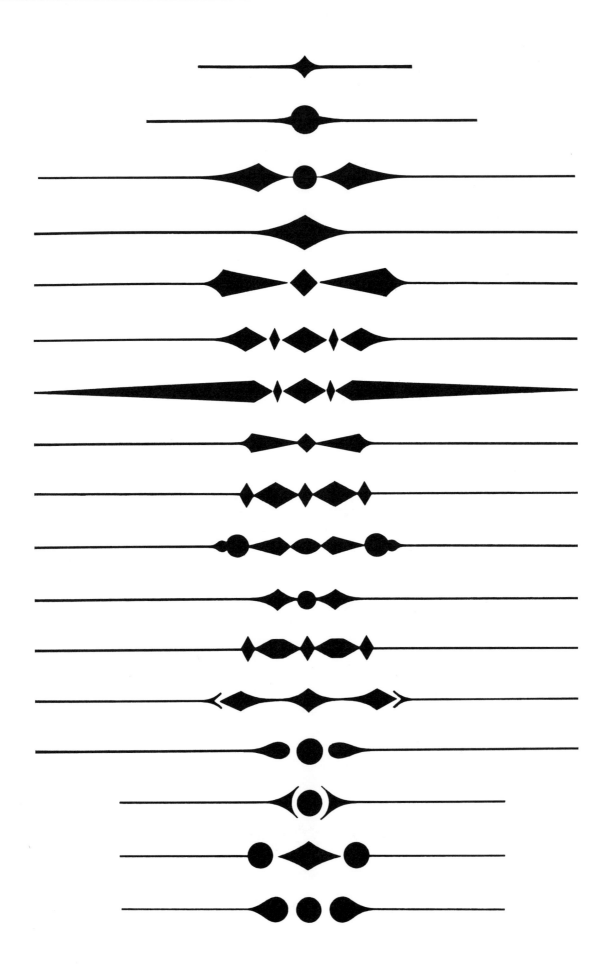

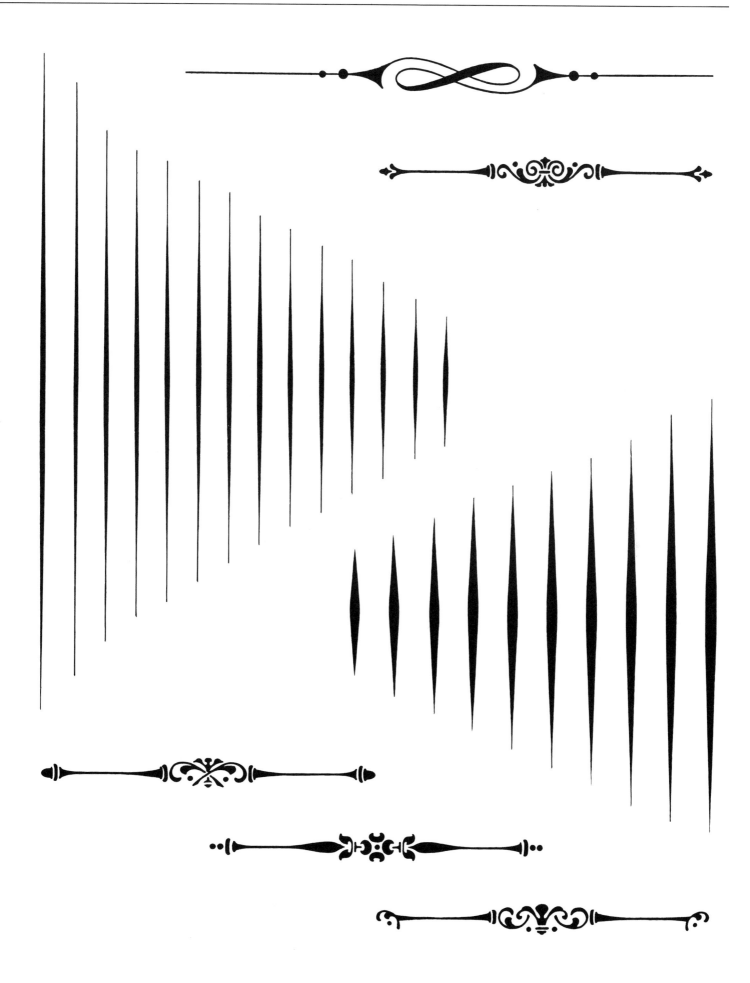

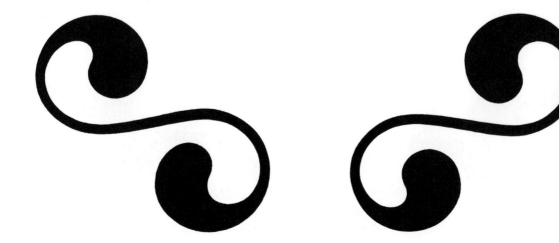

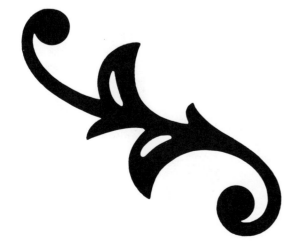

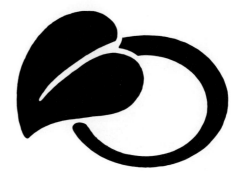

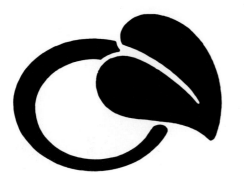

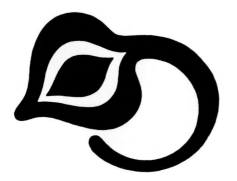

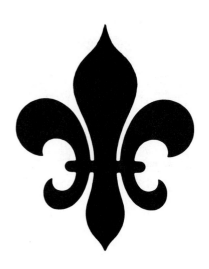

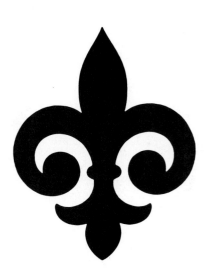

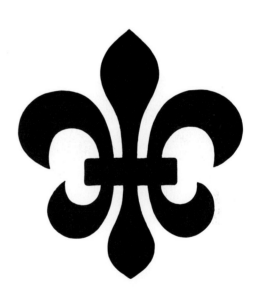

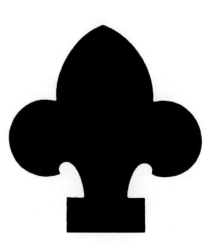

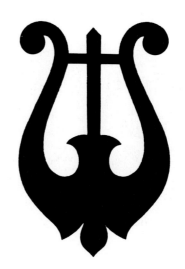

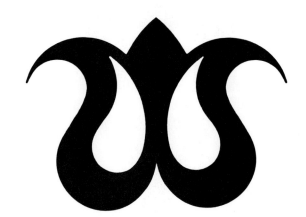

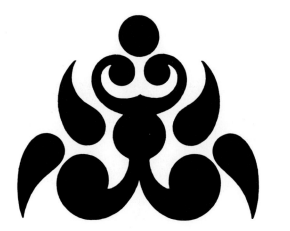

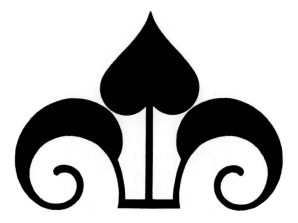

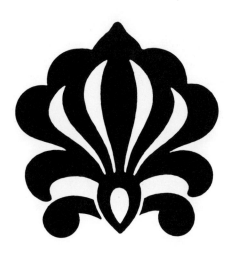

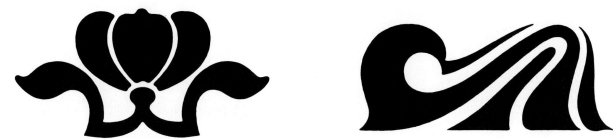

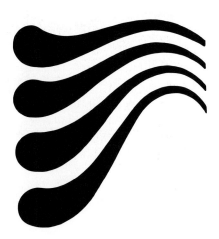

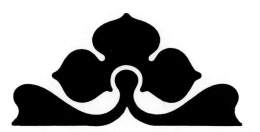

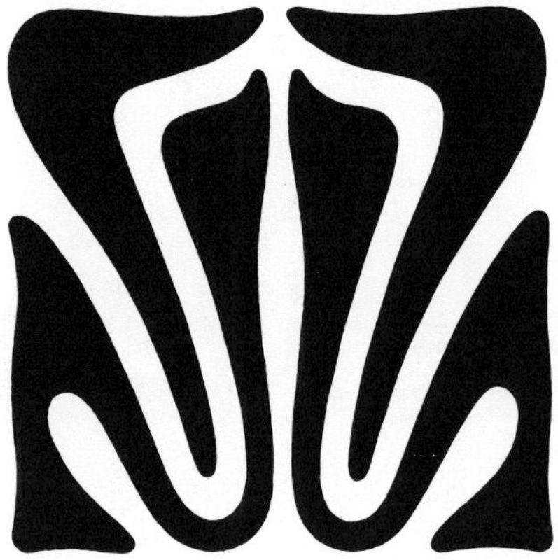

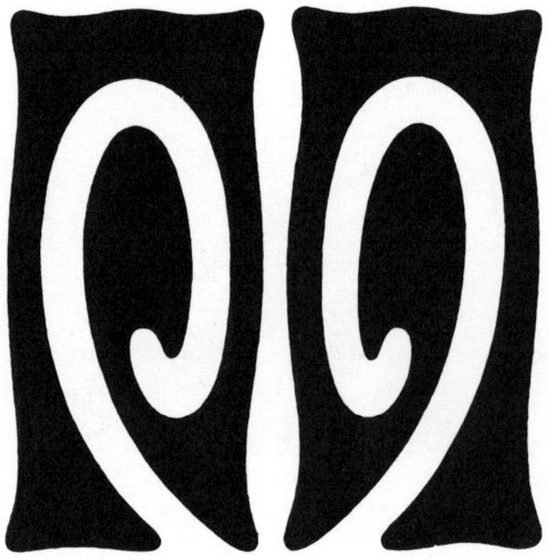

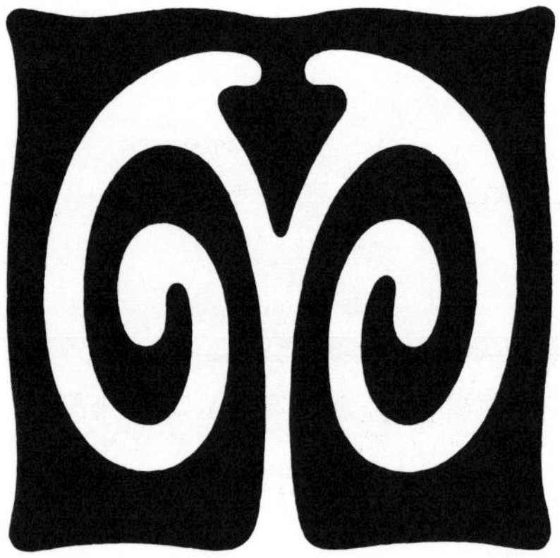

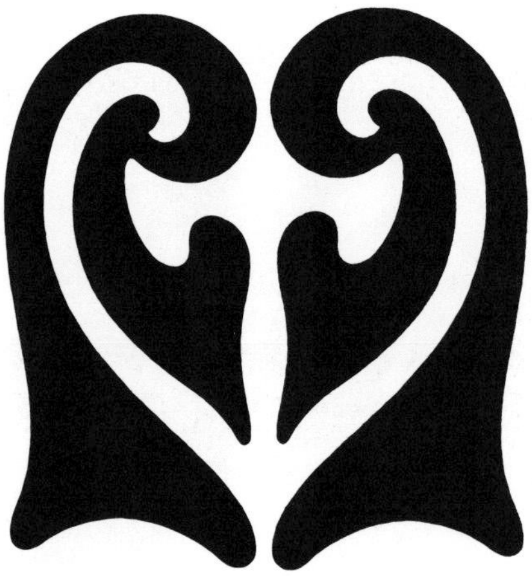

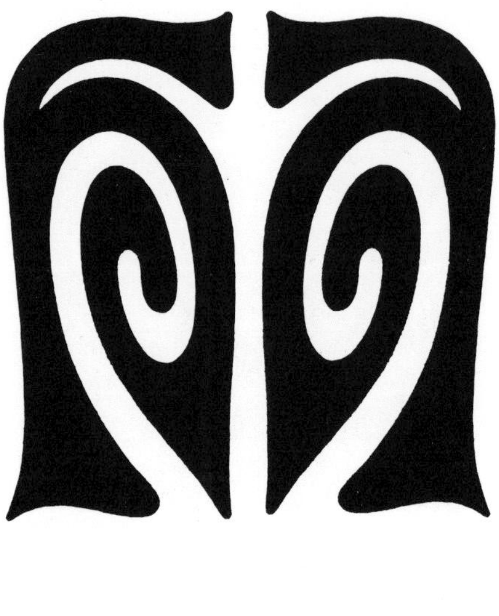

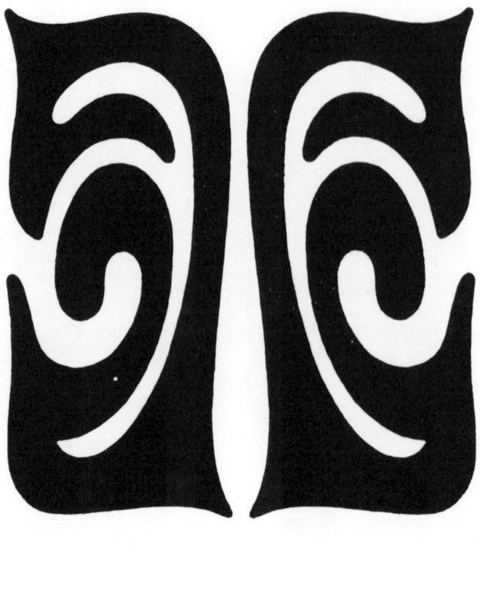

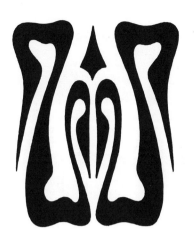